EMOTIONAL

PRISONS

Ken Gross

EMOTIONAL

PRISONS

BOOK TWO

PRISONS

Table of Contents

Acknowledgements

My most important acknowledgement must be to my parents, **Cyril and Barbara Gross**. They faced the impossible choice of abandoning me to save my life. In 1956, at three years old, I was diagnosed with Tuberculosis, which was most likely a death sentence back then in England. They faced the choice of putting me into a long-term sanatorium with the hope of healing, or keeping me living with them in London, a city that had a daily smog warning. They chose hope: how could I not acknowledge them!

Next, I'd like to acknowledge my wife, **Danita**. She is the one who has loved me and put up with my acting out: the 'crazy making' and the insecurity of living with an emotionally trapped person for so many years.

I must recognize my personal counselor, **Tim Mavergeorge**, who helped me to connect all the dots in my life and finally come to understand myself.

There have been pastors who had a part making unseen contributions to my soul, by influencing my thinking and they have added to this book in some way. **Tim Sledge, John Crawford, Alex Kennedy, Mike McGown and Jerry Edmonson.**

My men's prayer group, a place of refuge and safety for 19 years has been a constant source of acceptance, encouragement and strength.

I would also like to thank those that have helped with the editing process. Particularly **Kelly Wagler,** a fellow traveler in the difficult journey of life and **Kathy Trout**, my final editor, whose wonderful perfectionistic tendencies were very helpful at the end of the production of this book.

About the Author

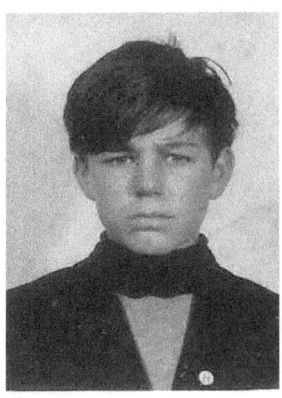

The author: age fourteen

Perhaps you note the serious demeanor.

Yes, my troubles started early. An intense child destined to struggle in life at 14. I was in my first emotional prison at age 15; the prison of false intimacy. I struggled with security, performance issues, acceptance and irresponsibility all my life.

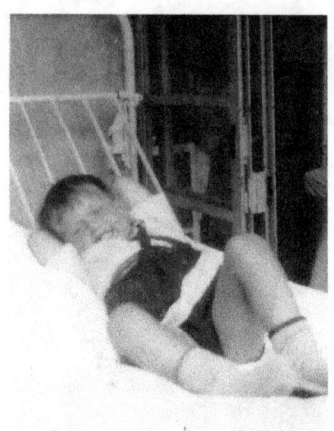

I was an abandoned child at three.

In this picture, I am seemingly so happy go lucky, yet I was living in a sanatorium with Tuberculosis In the picture, I had a white strap across me used to tie me down in bed at night, because I would get up and wake up the rest of the very sick children.

Finally, Christ got hold of me when I was ready and revealed me to myself; He told me of my troubles and explained how to be healed. The pages of this book, and the other two in the series, expose some of my life as they share the story of emotional prisons. *Ken Gross*

This is me now.

I was born in England in 1953 on an RAF base. My dad was 20 and mum 17. They had six more boys, but no girls, over the next few years; the last boy passed away within 24 hours of his birth. He was the brother I never met.

I contracted tuberculosis at three, was placed into long term care, and released 21 months later. I attended schools in my home town of Welwyn Garden City, about 20 miles north of London. I went to an elite high school (called a grammar school in the UK), attended the University of London through an outreach program, from which I obtained an undergraduate degree in Physics and Chemistry. A few years later I attended the University of Oklahoma, also through outreach, and received an MBA. I have been working in the financial services industry in the Houston area since 1986.

I currently reside in Katy, Texas with my wife and two dogs. I attend a local church, and run a ministry called Merimnao, which is mentioned on the next page.

Ministry

In 2009 I had a vision for ministry; a ministry for those trapped in emotional prisons, a ministry for those who were brokenhearted. In 2010 it was put into action. Thus was born "Merimnao" which is a Greek word that is often translated as burdens, anxieties, troubles or cares.

Go to www.merimnao.org to find out more about how we are helping others get out of their emotional prisons, overcome their compulsions and addictions, and move toward healing.

As the director of the ministry, I get to put a lot of the ideas laid out in the three "Emotional Prisons" books into practice. It is a fulfilling work, and I am blessed by God by being allowed to help Him as He heals people through it.

Ken Gross

Prologue

The whole idea of being trapped by emotions was birthed out of dealing with the dysfunctional behaviors in my own life. I actually wrote this book four years ago in 2008 and 2009. I got sidetracked by ministry, but it is time to publish my ideas.

The three books are simply constructed:

Book 1 – Emotional Prisons – Origins

I deal with what emotional prisons are and explain where they come from or how they are formed. I also give the reader a method of analyzing them, identifying the four major root emotional issues which stimulate their formation in a person's life.

Book 2 – Emotional Prisons - Prisons

In this book, I go into detail about some of the major emotional prisons that exist. Three of the chapters are about religious emotional prisons, including a candid look at the Christian version.

Book 3 – Emotional Prisons - Healing

In this book we look at the following considerations for healing:

1. Ten Principles of Healing
2. Twelve Barriers to Healing
3. Seven Healing Choices

I finish this last book with a chapter on conclusions I have drawn from writing the series.

The three books are ordered with a continuous numbering system for the chapters, this second book starts with Chapter 12, the third starts with Chapter 23.

EMOTIONAL PRISONS

BOOK 2

THE PRISONS

There are many emotional prisons; however there are some that seem to have more relevance to our culture; these are the prisons I've selected for discussion.

The first part of this book deals with the most common emotional prison there is; it is called religion. There was so much to cover that I had to break it down into three chapters; unconventional religions, conventional religions and religious Christianity.

This is followed by some clearly identifiable problems of life which are emotional prisons. Although I don't call them by these names we are going to look at compulsive sexual behaviors, chemical addictions, learned helplessness, gambling, codependence and perfectionism in some detail. Then I will spend a chapter on some more minor prisons and follow that up with an observational chapter which will lead from the prisons to the problem solutions or as I call it – healing.

The third book "Emotional Prisons – Healing" will go into detail about how and where to seek healing or release from our emotional prisons.

Throughout this book I will be referring to the SPAR analysis method from Chapter 8 of the first book, so it might be helpful to go back a take a quick look at it.

UNCONVENTIONAL RELIGIONS

It is an interesting view of Atheism, as a sort of "crutch" for those who can't stand the reality of God.
Tom Stoppard.

When I was writing my tentative outline and objective for this series of books, I asked myself a question, which maybe you could ask of yourself too. What is the emotional prison responsible for the most misery, over time, in our world? Quick answers came up, like drug addiction, drinking, sexual addiction or gambling. These answers, while all being big personal problems, didn't seem to hit the mark of "most misery." After some meditation on this subject; the answer was revealed to me, it was religion, not a specific religion, but religion in general. So that is where I decided to start this second book covering actual emotional prisons.

What is religion? If you look in a dictionary, you get answers like "belief in and worship of a supernatural being" or "a unified system of beliefs to live by." I found more than twenty different definitions, which is actually not helpful to this discussion, except to point out that there is no real agreement amongst language scholars on the subject. This meant that I had to come up with my own working definition, so here it is:

Religion is a system of beliefs in someone or something that we have zealous faith in, where our beliefs are put into actions.

This definition helps us to understand why religion can be so problematical. We can have zealous faith in a god (sometimes called a higher power), in a person, a cause, or an idea, but there is always an object of this zealous faith. I included the word "zealous" to ensure we all understand that religion involves fervency, or more than just a casual interest in something, it involves what can be described as an emotional buy-in. Religion further involves acting in accordance with those beliefs.

Because all religion has to have an emotional buy-in as well as an action component, all religions are able to contribute to an individual acting out of their emotions. You recall from the first book, "Emotional Prisons – Origins", that acting out is the point in our behavioral life at which we can start to become trapped in an emotional prison. Acting out usually involves the setting aside of rationality in an attempt to feel better about ourselves, and this is true in our religious pursuits too. Let me tell you about Susan (not her real name of course).

Susan went to the church I was attending a few years ago. She was married with two kids, but the marriage was shallow and unfulfilling, the kids were hard to handle and she was putting on weight. One evening during the week she watched a preacher on TV who said that problems could be overcome if you had enough faith in God. He then invited the audience to his next set of healing services at his church in Florida. So she decided to go! (We live near Houston, Texas.) She went, and surprise, she came back disappointed that her problems were not fixed. According to her, she had a great time of worship and believed that if she continued to attend by watching on TV and going whenever she could, things would get better.

So she did just that. Over a period of two years she went several times, spending money, time, and effort on fixing her problems. She definitely had an emotional buy-in to whatever message this preacher was handing out to his followers. It is a sad story that has been repeated in many ways, at many times, by many people. As she says it, she eventually concluded that she didn't have enough faith to fix her problems, and she became disillusioned with Christianity, because it didn't work. Fortunately, Susan got some better advice about life and turned back to her original belief system of conventional Christianity.

I used Susan's case as an example because it illustrates a side of the religion I am involved in which I believe causes problems in people's lives. I did this because I am going to discuss all the major world religions in the context of emotional prisons. So, I wanted to clearly state that even though I am a Christian, I acknowledge that parts of the Christian world have emotional prison issues too.

World Religions

There are literally hundreds of religions around the world, but in conventional wisdom it is generally recognized that there are five major religions. These are Buddhism, Christianity, Hinduism, Islam and Judaism. While these five fit with our definition of religion, there are

3

also other belief systems that do too. Remember, our definition says, "Religion is a system of beliefs in someone or something that we have zealous faith in, where our beliefs are put into actions." This means we must expand our list somewhat.

I don't want to spend much time on the discussion of whether a belief system is a religion or not, as it can develop into a pointless argument. It is more important to recognize that these few extra "religions" I'm going to list are significant belief systems that affect their adherents Soul activity, and therefore their behavior, and that they can be as zealous as any conventional "religious" person. I'm going to include Atheism, Communism and Occultism. With these three we now have a total of eight religions to look at using the SPAR method of analysis (Outlined in Chapter 8 of the first book).

Karl Marx, one of the most infamous philosophers of the modern era wrote this in 1884; "Religion is the sign of the oppressed creature, the sentiment of a heartless world, and the Soul of Soul-less conditions. It is the opium of the masses." While Marx was wrong about so many things, he was actually right about religion. Throughout human history religion has shown an amazing ability to medicate our troubled Souls much like opium can do. One of the big downsides of being medicated is that rationality sometimes is impaired, distorted or even eliminated, allowing the emotions of life to take over. It is this very problem which makes religion so dangerous to people while feeling so good.

In some of our look at religions we are going to see how this distortion of rationality, while substituting emotionally-guided decision-making through the Will, is played out. We will see how it affects people on an individual and collective level, and guides them into emotional prisons. In this chapter and the next two, we will look the eight religions; the first three (Atheism, Communism, and Occultism) in this chapter and the second four (Buddhism, Hinduism, Islam, and Judaism) in the next chapter. The third chapter will be dedicated to religious Christianity.

Atheism

What exactly is this, and why is it a religion? Quite simply, Atheism is the belief that there is no god or gods. People who are Atheists can be as zealous about their beliefs as any radical religionist. In fact, I've heard it said that if takes more faith to be an Atheist than to believe in a god. I like to ask this question of every Atheist I meet, "If there is no god, why do Atheists spend so much time talking about something they believe doesn't exist?" I have never received an answer that actually passes the honesty test. I'm going to come back to this issue below, but first I want to identify some of the most common forms of Atheism practiced around the world.

My knowledge and understanding of Atheism comes down to this in terms of what it is; there are three major forms of Atheism; they are Humanism, Secularism and Rationalism.

Humanism is a system of beliefs concerned mostly with human beings and their moral values that are gained from common experiences and human nature. What humanists cannot bring themselves to agree with or understand is that they have chosen man as their god. Humanists believe they are rational in those beliefs they hold, yet they cannot see that they get all their values, beliefs and attitudes from mankind. This infers that they revere and elevate man above all things, or put simply, they worship man. This makes man a god. We only have to look at the symbol or logo of the International Humanist and Ethical Union, the major worldwide humanist group, to see this. It is an "H" for Humanist with a "head" between two raised arms; the clear message is that of a person being adored, much like Jesus is pictured in many paintings.

The second major form of Atheism is Secularism. This is essentially a belief in the "system", which of course is manufactured by men. It doesn't look like that when you read the material which secularists generate, but that is what it is. They want to separate conventional religion from public life and keep it a private matter. They believe that the system will run better without any interference from those irrational faith-based people, meaning "religious folk." A big clue about the truth of what I am saying comes from the origins of the meaning of secular. Although it is used in a slightly different way today, the original meaning was in describing a religious person who was "in the world", meaning he or she was living a worldly life. Living a worldly life means today exactly what it meant then, living life using the rules of the world. This clearly implies a belief in those rules of the world as a religion, where the object of the belief is the "system."

Since rules differ from place to place around the world, secularists have different approaches to their religion in different locations, but they all have the belief in the "system." The United Nations organization can be thought of as an attempt to secularize the whole world.

5

The last major form of Atheism is Rationalism. This is a belief in rationality and the scientific method. The best example of this form of Atheism is Darwinism, which is a belief in evolution. The reason it is a good example is it helps us to see that rationalists worship nature in the broadest sense. They think everything revolves around physical and psychological laws, which is why they strongly reject the supernatural.

Whether Atheists agree or not, it is plain to me that they worship man, the world system, the created world or some combination of the three. Sometimes they even mix this worship up with conventional religion, and call themselves "Atheistic Christians", or "Secular Jews" or something similar in an attempt to hide their actual deep values, beliefs and attitudes.

A Personal Example

I used to be an Atheist, a position inherited from my father, who had a low level hostility to religion and God. Later, as a Christian, I spent some time trying to get him to see the hopelessness of his position, in the sense of having no future hope, which most conventional religions offer about life after death. He passed away declaring that there is no God. If you are a Christian reading this, you will understand how that grieves me. I say this because I want to make his passing more meaningful by telling the story of his life in the context of emotional prisons and Atheism, and utilizing the SPAR method.

Looking back, I have a great sense of sadness for my father. It seems to me that he really didn't stand a chance in life; you'll see why as I unfold the story. He was born during the time known as the Great Depression around the world and he was the baby of the family. He was doted on by his older siblings, cherished by my grandparents and was expected to be the last child as my grandmother was rapidly coming out of her child bearing years. Then it happened; a new child was conceived and born when my grandmother was 48 years old. Uncle Roy, as I came to know him later, was born with Down's Syndrome. He immediately became the center of attention, pushing my father out of his position as the youngest and most cherished child. He became emotionally abandoned!

It is hard to tell what might have been happening inside his immature Soul, but it got worse! The Second World War started, and for a period of time he was sent out of London, like a lot of kids, to avoid being at risk of being killed by the German bombs. To him, this was physical abandonment on top of the emotional abandonment. After the war, he met my mother and they got married. I was the first-born. This is when things got worse.

My mother had attended a local church school when she was growing up, so she wanted me to be christened, a Church of England version of infant baptism. My parents went to see the vicar (called the pastor here in the US) to arrange for this. Because my parents were forced to live on a military base outside of London, they were no longer residing in the parish, although they planned to go back there as soon as the tour of duty was over. The vicar refused to christen me because of that, even though he had known my mother for years. As it was told to me, that was the day my father decided there was no God. He had been abandoned by the church through this alleged man of God. He became an Atheist, and a hostile one!

Looking at what happened to my father we can see that by the time he was twenty years old he had experienced three forms of abandonment; emotional, physical and spiritual. Now you can probably agree with me that he really didn't stand a chance in life. (More on this below) We have talked about abandonment in Chapter 5 in the first book, and so I'm going straight to the result in his life. The SPAR factor that dominates my father's life is the "A" for Acceptance. This is where we ask the question, "How do I feel about myself, due to my perception of how others think and feel about me." A secondary SPAR factor is the "S" for Security, where the question is "How do I feel about myself?"

While I can't say for sure what my father felt during his life, I can put some pieces together, and create an incomplete but reasonably realistic picture of his internal Soul condition.

As a result of his childhood abandonment, he became hardened toward deep or intimate family connection in his Soul. While I never heard him say it, he had a very difficult time reaching out and loving someone, because he carried the fear of rejection. Interestingly though, his life demonstrated to me that he had the ability to love, which he showed through many of his actions. The incident with the church representative described compounded and cemented in his Heart that he was rejected as a person. Not only had everybody close to him, except his new wife, abandoned him, but also so had God, from his perspective. He learned that no one was trustworthy with the inner things; the things of the Heart.

When the chips were down, he could only rely on himself. It is only a small step from self-reliance to self-worship, which is one form of worship of man, which is humanism. Even though my father never said he was a Humanist, which is what he was. And that was his emotional prison!

As I have become more aware of how people really are, and how the Soul works I have come to appreciate my father much more. My father was disabled, not physically, but emotionally. He received an injury from his abandonment that he never recovered from and carried this Soul disability until the day he died. Yet, he stayed married to the same woman for 55 years, he provided for six boys, he was there with my mother as she lost the seventh, he placed me in hospital at age three and saved my life, and he did many other things. I said earlier, that he didn't stand a chance in life, and to me what he did accomplish was astonishing. I have to say that by the end I came to admire him, even though we disagreed about spiritual matters. Although he never said it, I know he loved my mother, my brothers and me. And I loved him.

The Prison of Atheism

The core problem for Atheists is that they believe man is everything. Their whole set of values, beliefs and attitudes revolve around this. And every Atheist will deny that this is true of their religion. It doesn't matter whether an Atheist is a Humanist, a Secularist or a Rationalist; man, meaning the human race, has to be good and perfect. This is where the trap gets sprung. Man is not good and perfect, just read the front page of a newspaper to discover that. In fact, man is quite clearly bad, and often evil, and definitely imperfect. Atheists need man to become more perfect over time, which they call evolution, in order for their beliefs to be accurate. Again, just look at history, man has been involved in murder since the beginning of time; nothing has changed about man's nature.

The prison of Atheism is the belief structure. When the core belief in man is challenged by a fact, such as men doing evil things, they have to come up with some kind of excuse for why their beliefs have failed. Consider the Atheists belief in macro-evolution (Darwinism). Darwin first postulated this theory in 1859, and to this date 2013, no record has been found of a macro change in any species. That is 154 years of failure! Do Atheists say there is something wrong with their faith? No! Do they acknowledge that one of their most cherished beliefs is in crisis?

8

No! Do they even admit that their best thinking shows serious flaws? No! They are trapped by their strongly held convictions that they are right and everybody who doesn't agree is wrong.

So what do they do about it? Some of them write books, and attack others and their beliefs to prove that the Atheist view is right. It is pathetic that very intelligent people can put so much time and effort into book writing and deny facts in order to feel good about themselves. This is primarily the SPAR factor of Performance at work, and secondarily the SPAR factor of Acceptance.

Some Atheists indulge in some more extreme and dysfunctional behavior. I'm thinking here of protestors, bombers, and some terrorists. We've all seen the news about animal rights activists throwing paint over celebrities who wear fur, or the eco-terrorists who blow up someone else's property to stop some kind of legitimate activity. These people are committing immoral acts because of their beliefs. For this kind of action to occur the SPAR factor "R" for Responsibility is evident. Remember that the salient question here is, "How do I feel about myself, due to my ability to meet certain standards?" It is also possible that the Acceptance factor is at work, since people who do this are usually part of a group where beliefs and actions are part of getting and staying accepted.

In the broadest sense Atheists are similar to addicts. They all act out of their emotions because of their values, beliefs and attitudes. But, they are just as trapped!

Communism

Communism is the next religion I want to cover. It is commonly thought of as an example of Atheism, but it is not. This is because it does not have mankind, a system, or the natural world as the object of worship around which a belief system is built and acted upon. Rather, Communism is a belief system built around ideology, which is what makes it so dangerous. Many actions have been carried out in the name of this ideology, and there has been a lot of evil done because of it.

While I am not going to attempt to provide a history of Communism, I do want to say something about it. The religion of Communism, as practiced in our world has been responsible for more deaths than any other religion. Verify that what I have said is accurate for yourself and you will find that this is true. Just look at what every major communist state has done. It is estimated that in Russia over 60 million people were killed, in China it is estimated to be 50 million, an in Cambodia, communism killed 3 million. I could go on but I won't. There is clearly something wrong with this picture, and what is it? I am going to attempt to answer this issue.

To explain this awful situation I'll use the SPAR method of looking at the actions of the leaders of communist society, and their close followers who took the orders and carried out the policies that led to all these deaths.

First, let us look at the leaders, remembering that these are people having a Soul and subject to the same operational characteristics we looked at in the first four chapters of the first book. At some level these leaders had values, beliefs and attitudes that were derived from the ideology of Communism. All of them combined whatever knowledge, understanding, and wisdom they had accumulated with these values, beliefs and attitudes and made choices to adopt communism as their religion. This religion was then, in every case that I know of, forced on the population of the country, and each of them became a one political party state. The party was the Communist party, and it was the only party allowed, much like Islam is now in some countries.

The leaders were an insecure bunch! They did not allow significant dissent, and severely punished it by imprisonment or death. They did not accept that there might be other ways of dealing with problems than complete submission to the will of the party, which was, of course, the leaders. The leaders were firmly under the control of their emotions which sprang from how they dealt with the SPAR Responsibility factor. Remember that this is the factor that deals with the question, "How do I feel about myself, due to my ability to meet specific standards?" The standards in question were those originally laid out by Marx, Engels and others. These standards included standards of property ownership, standards of lack of class division, standards of economic parity, and most ominously standards of methods of goal achievement. It is that last one which was the problem.

The leader trying to meet the standards of methods had to resort to some seemingly irrational choices. (Remember choice is a characteristic of the Will.) They had to centrally plan economic activity, which leads to falling economic efficiency and productivity. They had to close down fully functional farms and change them into something else. They took people off the land where they had lived for centuries and put them in factory apartments. Worst of all, they took people who spoke against the belief system and killed them, thereby removing the "problem." All of this happened because the leaders didn't feel secure enough to allow others to have differences with them.

The followers of these leaders had other issues. They were most likely dealing with all four SPAR factors. They too were insecure, but they were also performance-driven (doing a good job for the party). They probably sought acceptance, and so engaged in people-pleasing activity for the leaders, including carrying out the orders to kill the "problems." Some of them may also have had ambitions to become leaders, and so they were also engaged in "staying pure" by keeping themselves and their party up to those pesky standards.

All in all, Communism is a miserable religion that fails to persuade or convince the people of the world that their way is "the way." Those that followed it certainly acted out of their emotions, with terrible results. Communists are as stuck in an emotional prison as any perpetual drunk.

Occultism

I must confess that this religion is the most difficult to get one's head around. There are so many ways this is perceived, and so many ways the subject is defined. Elements of these definitions include secrecy, unknown forces, supernatural powers, deceit, mysticism and concealment. Just saying those words gives us a flavor of what we are looking at with this religion. In a dictionary, Occultism is primarily thought of as study of the occult, but it is more than that.

To figure out what it is, I must first remind us of what a religion is. "Religion is a system of beliefs in someone or something that we have zealous faith in, where our beliefs are put into actions." In this case the "someone or something", the object of this religion, is the Occult, and that is where we start to look at the emotional prison of Occultism. The Occult seems to have been around for all of human history and is comprised of many different aspects. I found plenty of examples of these different aspects of the Occult and I'll list a few here:

- **Satanism, Shamanism and Séances**
- **Witchcraft, Wicca and Voodoo**
- **Tantra, Rosicrucionism and Psychicism**

- **Black Magic, Demonology and Druidism**

When we take a look at these we can see some common themes. We can see belief in the supernatural, belief in unknown powers, belief in the ability to make things happen that violate natural laws, belief in talking to the dead, and belief in the ability to get special revelation at will. Trying to take all these things into account I am going to use the following definition of Occultism:

- **Occultism is the belief in, worship of, and activity around mostly unknown and unseen beings, objects and practices of a supernatural nature.**

To see what God thinks, I think it would be appropriate here to take a look at a passage of scripture that relates to this whole subject.

Dt 18:9-12 - When you enter the land which the Lord your God gives you, you shall not learn to imitate the detestable things of those nations. There shall not be found among you anyone who makes his son or his daughter pass through the fire, one who uses divination, one who practices witchcraft, or one who interprets omens, or a sorcerer, or one who casts a spell, or a medium, or a spiritist, or one who calls up the dead. For whoever does these things is detestable to the Lord; and because of these detestable things the Lord your God will drive them out before you.

Without getting in too deep here, we can say that God lists some practices He calls detestable, performed by people He calls detestable, these are:

- One who makes his son or daughter pass through the fire; which is human sacrifice of children.
- One who uses divination, which is foretelling future events, ostensibly through a supernatural power. (Like a palm or tarot card reader)
- One who practices witchcraft, which is black magic.
- One who interprets omens.
- One who is a sorcerer, which is a person who exercises supernatural power over others.
- One who casts a spell, a person who enchants others.
- One who is a medium. That is a person who is thought to communicate with the spirits of the dead.

- One who is a spiritist, a person who consults with supernatural beings.
- One who calls up the dead, somebody who revives, or attempts to revive, dead people.

That list is a reasonably comprehensive list of occultists, or people who practice the religion of occultism. The question that faces us is this, "Why would any person engage in any of these activities?" When we look at what an occultist is trying to accomplish, and why they may be engaging in these practices, we get some idea of the SPAR factors that are at work.

What is an occultist trying to accomplish? I see three basic goals here:

1. Trying to get favors from some unknown supernatural entity.
2. Trying to demonstrate that they, the occultists, have mysterious powers.
3. Trying to exercise supernatural control in their life, for the purpose of having power over circumstances or other people.

The motives behind these three goals are what indicates what is going on within the Soul of these occultists.

First, or number one on the list, when a person feels the necessity to do something outrageous like the child sacrifice we mentioned above, there is something seriously wrong. There are some people who believe that the modern day scourge of abortion is child sacrifice. Back in biblical times people used to throw their young children, often their newborns, into a fire to appease a god or if the child was the first born, to ask for fertility. That seems crazy to us today, and barbaric, but don't we do it now? So many children are killed in the mother's womb as a sacrifice to convenience, and we made it legal and called it abortion on demand.

What goes on inside the Soul of someone who makes a sacrifice (this can also be called a gift) to unknown gods? Obviously, they believe they will receive a blessing of some kind in return, even if that only means they will not receive a curse. The inevitable end of this is disappointment, which means the outcome and the expectation didn't match up. Even if some blessing enters the occultist's life, eventually failure of the unknown god to produce will result. This can lead to increased sacrifice, in quantity, frequency, or seriousness, which leads to more problems.

When a person is feeling insecure, the "S" in SPAR, they are likely to act out of the emotion generated from their belief that this unknown god will meet their needs or desires. As this god fails them, the insecurity gets worse, and the other three SPAR factors start to kick in. The occultist who practices sacrifice, or giving, to unknown gods begins to feel bad about themselves in new ways. They feel that their sacrificial abilities are not good enough; the "P" in SPAR is at work. They may also feel rejected by the unknown god; the "A" in SPAR is at work. Finally, this poor misguided person may feel that they are not sacrificing in quite the right way or perhaps not saying the right words; the 'R' from SPAR is working here. Can you see how trapped this person is because of their emotional responses to the failure of their sacrifice or giving?

The second goal, which is where an Occultist is trying to demonstrate that they have mysterious powers, ratchets up the whole insanity of this religion. The core problem here is, again, personal insecurity. An individual dabbling in things like reading palms or tarot cards, or maybe acting as a medium, is trying to feel important, because they are not secure within themselves. It is probably true that we all have some of that, but not many of us resort to Occultist behavior to medicate our feelings of insecurity. When a person doing these things starts to provide a service to others, sometimes for money, they are going one step further, and seeking acceptance from others, the "A" from SPAR. Then as this doesn't satisfy their emotional cravings, they move on to the "hamster wheel" seeking a deeper level of performance in their activities; the "P" in SPAR.

This results in their taking more risk in their Occultist religion, seeking that always-elusive spiritual revelation so they can feel better about themselves. Since they are dealing with things they don't understand, the danger becomes more and more acute. It can be hard to get connected with what that means so I'll paint a word picture. If I gave you a box full of snakes, and then said, "Place this blindfold on and put your hands in it", would you? Probably not, because you know enough to understand that it could be dangerous. The Occultist trying to demonstrate their mysterious powers is doing the equivalent of putting the hands of their Soul into a box of spiritual snakes while being unable to see anything. Some of these spiritual snakes may not seem to harm you, but there are some poisonous ones in there!

Dabbling in this stuff is as much an emotional prison as drugs or pornography and will drag a person down in much the same way. The end point will be a deep dungeon of despair, and it will be hard to overcome such a stronghold of misery in someone's life.

The last goal, the most dangerous, is that of exercising supernatural control in one's life, for the purpose of having power over others. This may be one of the least wise choices any human can make. The person who does this is deliberately engaging the supernatural, believing that they can control it and use it for their own benefit. Just how dumb can a person be? Trying to link up with someone or something you cannot know or understand, for the purpose of using "them" or "it", has got to be one of the most insane acts that an individual can perform. In my box of snakes analogy, it is like trying to put your hands in, while blindfolded, and picking out a Cobra, which you plan to use to control others.

What could possibly be driving such a dangerous behavior? At its deepest root, it is the "A" of SPAR; it is Acceptance. This person so desperately wants to be accepted that they will do this kind of acting out. The strange thinking that goes on here is very simple. If I can control others, they will have to accept me. So as to clearly state the danger of this practice, let us spend just a line or two on it. Of the three biggest mass murderers of the twentieth century, at least two, Hitler and Stalin, were heavily involved in the Occult. The third, Mao Tse Tung, was thought to be, but the evidence is sketchy.

While I cannot treat this subject with the space, time and depth it deserves, I hope that as you have read what I did write, you are challenged. Messing around with the occult in any way is foolishness and at its worst, highly dangerous. If you are personally involved in such things, stop. Quit reading horoscopes, don't go to palm readers, don't attend séances, keep away from mediums or spiritists, and don't associate with people who do these things. Occultism is a deep and dark emotional prison.

CONVENTIONAL RELIGIONS

*Men never do evil so completely and cheerfully as when they do it from
a religious conviction.*
Blaise Pascal

Since this is the second of three chapters dealing with the general topic
of religion as an emotional prison, I think it would be good to remind
ourselves what religion is.

**Religion is a system of beliefs in someone or something that we have
zealous faith in, where our beliefs are put into actions.**

In the previous chapter we looked at the first three religions of Atheism,
Communism and Occultism. Now we are going to move to the next
four, which might be thought of as more conventional religions. We will
start with Buddhism, then look at Hinduism and move on to two of the
three monotheistic religions of Islam and Judaism; Christianity will be
looked at in the following chapter.

Buddhism

There are some who contest the fact that Buddhism is a religion. Well to
put this to rest let us look at what the World Buddhist Sangha Council
said at their first meeting. "Buddha is our only master." That was their
first point; the second was "We take refuge in the Buddha." They have a
holy book, which is usually called the "Pali Canon", or "Tritaka", a
collection of early Buddhist teachings. Buddhists have system of beliefs
based on the "Four Noble Truths" which center around suffering, its
origins, consequences, meaning and purposes. Understanding suffering
leads to the path of enlightenment. While on the path of enlightenment,
there are three ways to actually attain it that are determined by your
ability or capacity. The highest level of enlightenment is "Samyak-Sam-
Buddha", which gives you the ability to save others.

To me these teachings and practices have all the elements of religion, an
object of worship (Buddha), a system of beliefs (Trikata), and activities

because of those beliefs (path of enlightenment). In this religion we see something new, the concept of salvation, meaning that all humans need to be saved from something. For Buddhists it is suffering. Once saved the Buddhist can reach a place called Nirvana, which is a state of total blessedness, or enlightenment. In the language I have been using in this book, this would be labeled a "Soul condition", much like a "euphoric state" might be called a Soul condition. It is my opinion that it is the "salvation from suffering" goal of Nirvana, which makes Buddhism so appealing to so many people. It is also the "salvation from suffering" that is the reason this religion directs so many people into an emotional prison. Let's look at how this happens.

There is no doubt that people suffer, and it is probably thought of as common to all men, meaning that everybody suffers. I want to acknowledge that there is physical suffering in the world, but also say that it does not mean all men are suffering physically at all times. While Buddhism does address physical suffering, the suffering Buddhism primarily deals with is the suffering of the Soul, which can also be said of this whole book series to a certain extent.

From the perspective of an outsider, Buddhism can be very attractive as it provides a way of dealing with painful emotions, which it calls suffering. The whole idea is to raise the consciousness of the Soul to the point where the Mind (Knowledge, Understanding and Wisdom) dominates Soul activity and the Soul feels peace. Peace for the Buddhist is the absence of suffering. This is actually a powerful denial of emotions. It involves the Mind and the Will (Choice, Control and Gateway) suppressing the actual feelings that get generated by the Soul.

The four noble truths and the path to enlightenment are placed in the Heart as beliefs to the extent that they overrule any truths which contradict them. An example is the belief in reincarnation. There is no conclusive evidence that any person has been reincarnated, ever. If a Buddhist accepted this truth, they would have to deny their belief system.

Now let us take a look at Buddhists through the SPAR analysis. The core problem a person who engages in this religion faces is that they can only feel okay with themselves if they meet certain standards. This is the "R" in SPAR, where we answer the question, "How do I feel about myself, due to my ability to meet certain standards?" What are these standards? Let me list them and you will see how easy it is to think that this religion is a set-up for failure.

17

- The Four Noble Truths
- The Five Skandhas
- The Six Realms
- The Eightfold Path

When a Buddhist actually meets all the standards and achieves Nirvana, they have reached the top; there is nothing else to do. If a Buddhist fails at some level, they get reincarnated, and get another shot at it. Since the truth is that reincarnation does not ever happen, this whole process leads to the very thing it is trying to deal with; suffering. I am referring to the suffering induced into the Soul by the failure to meet certain standards.

How can I be so sure about this? I simply look at societies where Buddhism is the dominant religion and ask, have they achieved a lower level of suffering than any other societies? The answer is, no!

There are some Buddhists who are able to suppress or deny their feelings and achieve some level of peace, but the same can be said of other religious mechanisms too. It is my contention that, generally speaking, Buddhism actually traps people in suffering. it is an emotional prison in its own right.

Hinduism

There is no doubt that this religion is a bona fide one. It has all the three major characteristics; object(s) of worship, a belief system, and activity to support and promote the belief system. This may come as a surprise to some Christians but Hinduism has some commonalities with Christianity. Common themes are:

- Both have a trinity
- Both separate God and man
- Both acknowledge that man is a physical being with a Soul
- Both emphasize personal worship
- Both stress the importance of religious duties
- Both have a creation story

However, there are also major differences:

- Hinduism has many paths to God, Christianity has one

- Hinduism has many minor gods, Christianity does not
- Hinduism separates people into castes, Christianity says all are equal
- Hinduism allows idol worship, Christianity does not
- Hinduism allows for reincarnation, Christianity says we only have one life

When I have looked at Hinduism it seems that the Hindus took the basic truths of Christianity and altered them. Of course that cannot be accurate because Hinduism was shaped well before the birth of Christ. Unless your understanding of Christianity allows you to accept that it has always existed, but we (mankind) did not have a name for it. That of course is a question for theologians to work out, but it does shed light on this religion of Hinduism.

I think people who seriously follow this religion are struggling with all four of the SPAR factors. In particular the "A" for acceptance, the reality of the caste system of Hinduism is all about acceptance, and where a person fits in to society. The emphasis on religious duties such as daily worship, non-violence and doing good deeds, is from the "P" of performance. The multitude of gods is due to the many rules, regulations and unspoken standards, leading to the "R" factor, responsibility, being important. Just choose the god that works for you and you'll feel okay.

It seems reasonably obvious that if a Hindu is serious about his or her faith, they are on a permanent treadmill and have no rest for their Soul. There is a constant worry about your family being forced down the caste levels to become less of a person. There is also a constant challenge in trying to move up to a higher level of privilege. This religion is also a trap for a Soul. The trap is a combination of failure to perform, fear of rejection, and a sense of inadequacy.

Islam

Islam is also definitely a religion, having an object of worship (Allah), a belief system (laid out in the Koran and Hadith) and activity (Sunnah – way of life) to support the system. It is often called one of the world's great religions, a statement I don't support. I find it to be very dysfunctional in how it is followed.

I think it is possible that I am going to annoy some Moslems by what I say here. I have read the Koran, the Islamic holy book, a couple of times and I find it to be a chaotic piece of literature. It is very clear that the deity known as Allah in the Koran is not the same as the God of the Bible. I am going to offer only one piece of evidence for this statement, although there are many, but this is a very profound thing.

Islam, the classical Arabic name of the religion, is translated into English as meaning "submission." The god of the Moslem religion, Allah, demands complete submission, just because he says so. The God of the Bible does not demand submission, He expects obedience of those that say they follow Him, but He allows freedom of choice in this. This says everything anyone really needs to know. Allah is a control freak, and God is not, so they cannot be the same. It is the control freak nature of their god that is the major contributor to Moslems getting emotionally trapped.

Just looking at some of the actions taken by Moslems gives us a picture of some of the emotional problems this religion leads to. I want to start with how they are to treat unbelievers; let us see what their holy book says in Sura (a chapter of the Koran) Five verses 33-34:

The punishment of those who wage war against Allah and His apostle and strive to make mischief in the land is only this, that they should be murdered or crucified or their hands and their feet should be cut off on opposite sides or they should be imprisoned; this shall be as a disgrace for them in this world, and in the hereafter they shall have a grievous chastisement, except those who repent before you have them in your power; so know that Allah is Forgiving, Merciful. (From the University of Michigan translation)

This is a direct command to make war against, and kill or maim, people that don't follow Islam, unless they convert. This is how the religion was propagated in its early years. It is also interesting that modern day Jihadists, who are the Moslems who follow this command, almost always call on their potential victims to convert and thereby avoid the violence.

For those that think the Islam we are seeing is new and different, and will pass from its current state to something better, I am going to offer the following. It is a quote from Sir Winston Churchill made in one of his early writings, "The River War", Volume II, published in 1899, making it over 100 years old.

"How dreadful are the curses which Mohammedanism lays on its votaries! Besides the fanatical frenzy, which is as dangerous in a man as hydrophobia in a dog, there is this fearful fatalistic apathy. The effects are apparent in many countries. Improvident habits, slovenly systems of agriculture, sluggish methods of commerce, and insecurity of property exist wherever the followers of the Prophet rule or live. A degraded sensualism deprives this life of its grace and refinement; the next of its dignity and sanctity. The fact that in Mohammedan law every woman must belong to some man as his absolute property, either as a child, a wife, or a concubine, must delay the final extinction of slavery until the faith of Islam has ceased to be a great power among men. Individual Moslems may show splendid qualities - but the influence of the religion paralyses the social development of those who follow it. No stronger retrograde force exists in the world. Far from being moribund, Mohammedanism is a militant and proselytizing faith. It has already spread throughout Central Africa, raising fearless warriors at every step; and were it not that Christianity is sheltered in the strong arms of science, the science against which it had vainly struggled, the civilisation of modern Europe might fall, as fell the civilisation of ancient Rome."

There is a phrase in this quote that is such a truth, "the influence of the religion paralyses the social development of those that follow it." This has always been true, and honesty dictates that when we look at what Islam does to its followers, we acknowledge that there is something terribly wrong. Islam is a danger to the whole world, because it depraves the Souls of those who follow it. Let us look at some of the behaviors that are acceptable under Islam. I am simply going to list them here, but there is plenty of support for my observations available in Islamic literature and in scholarly books on the Islamic faith. The Internet can also provide a more casual observer with a great deal of information on this subject.

- Subjugation of women
- Murder of unbelievers
- Breaking of contracts
- Lying to unbelievers
- Killing apostates
- Stoning female adulterers or suspected adulterers
- Revenge killings
- Stealing

What kind of religion, or belief system, allows murder, lying, cheating and stealing? The kind that corrupts the Soul of its followers!

I lived in Saudi Arabia, the home of Islam, for seven years. It was during the first oil boom when significant amounts of money were pouring in to the country. But there was abject poverty everywhere. The wealth was being held by the ruling powers. I knew many Moslems, mostly Saudi men, some Pakistanis, Lebanese and Palestinians. On a one-on-one basis these were good people, but once you began to talk about religious things, an air of militancy arose. At the time, I just blew it off as differences in culture. I was an Atheist and I really couldn't see what was in front of me, spiritually speaking. But it was the power of Islam at work. Let us look at what happens to a person's Soul within Islam, realizing that I can only speak in generalizations. The reason for this is that Islam twists the Soul so badly that I don't have space in this book to deal with the subject in great depth.

First, we must understand that Islam is a religion of submission. This means that every Soul is subjected to constant pressure to conform to the beliefs of the religion. From the earliest days of a person's life, they constantly receive this message; it is forced into the gateway of the Soul and placed into the Heart as a belief (Islam is all things). The individual then assumes values and attitudes which reinforce that belief. In our culture we would call it brain washing, although it ought to be called "Heart corrupting." Any resistance to Islam in a child is squashed, sometimes with considerable violence.

The factual evidence of the inability of the religion to improve the material or psychological state of its followers is strong. This puts the leaders of the religion in a place where they have to obfuscate truth and replace it with a lie. The lie is that the rest of the world is morally corrupt, and pure Islam is the only way to save yourself. At the individual level, the child, adolescent and adult Souls of Moslems are receiving this message through their gateway on a constant and consistent basis. This constant "propaganda", for that is what it is, causes a very typical response found in many similar situations. The response is something I call externalizing, which means that instead of looking inside and being honest about one's Soul condition, we look outside. It is actually very powerful, as it allows a person to blame everybody else for his or her own problems. It is also about as dishonest as a Soul can get.

This dishonesty becomes the pathway to more problems. When something comes up that contradicts Islam and its teachings, dishonesty requires it to be dealt with harshly to eliminate it. Generally speaking, there is no real attempt in the Soul of a Moslem to seek the truth. In the extreme, a Moslem will kill someone who shines the light of truth on his or her behavior and exposes lies or some form of behavioral dichotomy. A good example is the Danish cartoon incident of 2007. This is where there were riots over some cartoons printed in a Danish newspaper about the prophet of Islam, Mohammed. The light of truth was shone on aspects of Islam and how it is followed or practiced. People rioted, some of them got killed. A "fatwa", which is an Islamic religious judgment over something, was issued to kill the cartoonists. The problem was not the cartoons, it was that the truth of Islam was exposed, and they didn't like it. Instead of addressing the issue, and using factual evidence and reason, they try to eliminate the messengers of the truth.

Now let's look, using the SPAR method, at what goes on to cause good people to do these things we have been talking about. I want to emphasize here that within the Moslem world, and from a human perspective, there are both good and bad people, remembering that this is true of all cultures or social groups. There is something that goes on inside this religion which causes good individuals to violate their own natural humanity. What is it?

From the SPAR perspective, the answer is simple yet complex. It is simple in that answering the question gives me a straightforward response, and complex because it has many facets, nuances or intricacies to it. The response is this; Moslems are deeply insecure. Let us unpack that!

In thinking about what goes on in the Souls of individuals following Islamic beliefs, I came to realize that all four SPAR factors are at work. I also began to develop an understanding that the whole Islamic world is in the grip of fears, laziness born out of fatalism and an inability to search for truth stemming from blind submission. So let us look at these things, beginning with the SPAR factor of "Security."

"Security", if you recall from Chapter 8, is all about answering the question, "How do I feel about myself?" For the follower of Islam this is a problem. There is nothing in Islamic teachings, which I know of, that speaks to the inherent value of man. If man has no value, he or she spends each day with a belief in their Heart which is something like this,

"I am worthless." It is of high importance for us to understand this message and what it does to the Soul of a Moslem.

When any person has a set of beliefs, values and attitudes in their Heart that state "I am worthless", it will lead them to feelings of worthlessness (obviously), but also hopelessness, despair, uselessness and inadequacy. Having perspective here is important. We need to understand that this is a systemic cultural truth about followers of Islam. While individual Moslems may have been able to overcome this barrier to a healthy life, most Moslems have not, nor will they ever as long as they adhere to the teachings of the Koran. With the pervasiveness of feelings of worthlessness, should it be a surprise how Moslems act out? Let us look at some of the behaviors of Moslems that are examples of this sense of worthlessness or insecurity.

One of the biggest is the inability of Moslems to give equal value to women and men. It is even codified in their laws, called Sharia Law, that women have half the value a man has in a court situation. Consider also that when a woman is raped, she needs three male witnesses to be able to prosecute the rapist. Is that equal protection under the law, no! When I lived in Saudi Arabia I often saw women sitting in the back of a pick up as it sped down the road in 120-degree heat. In the front may be the kids, but I also saw small animals, and empty seats. How valuable can women feel about themselves in that culture?

The next acting out behavior showing a lack of value for man is that of Islamic martyrdom. Before Islam even existed there were martyrs, and they were traditionally found in the Christian world. A martyr, under its current use in language, is someone who dies for his or her religious beliefs by choice, but doesn't really want to. In the Islamic world, a martyr is also someone who dies for his or her religious beliefs by choice, but in this case they want to. It might seem like a subtle difference, but it is not. In the first case the person is willing to die, but values their life. In the Islamic case, they are willing to die, but do not value their life. This breeds a culture of death, the best example of which is the suicide bomber that we consistently hear about. I have seen many attempts to explain this away, such as economic despair or political hopelessness. They have the emotional aspect right, but not the true origin. The origin of this problem is the religion that teaches that life and people have no or limited value.

My third and last example of these behaviors which show the inability of the Moslem world to value man is discrimination. The Moslem discriminates as a belief; they believe that it is acceptable to segregate and show favor between people groups. The most obvious is between Moslems and non-Moslems. Moslem governments are legally allowed to tax Moslems at one rate, and non-Moslems at a higher rate. Non-Moslems have lower levels of legal recourse in court, and their testimony has less value. While Moslems will deny this, they still practice slavery, and regard it as acceptable. The biggest public display of discrimination is their attitude toward the Jews. The "holy men" of Islam frequently call them "pigs" and "apes", and routinely call for the extermination of the entire Jewish race.

After looking at the insecurity endemic in the Moslem world, let's move on to the "P", in SPAR, for Performance. This is where we ask the question, "How do I feel about myself, due to what I do?" This is a very interesting aspect of the Islamic world. I want to begin this part of our look at performance by asking the question, "What significant achievements or discoveries have come out of the Islamic world since the time Mohammed the prophet delivered Allah's messages?" The answer is very little! As I researched this issue, I came across claims of great scientific, medicinal, agricultural and architectural works. Looking deeper though we find that the real successes came from taking other peoples creativity and incorporating it into its own culture. In fact, the Moslem world has a definite bias against creativity, particularly in the arts. Productivity doesn't seem to be a virtue nor is it promoted in this culture.

It is this lack of drive that is very interesting to me. There is no lack of talent or intellectual capability in the people within this culture. There just seems to be some way that what ought to be a large amount of creative or industrious talent is held back or subdued. I have come to picture this phenomenon as strangely unique to the Moslem world. This is because it doesn't have a parallel anywhere else that I know of. There is something within the Islamic world system that discourages individuality in endeavor, and it appears to me to be a culture wide problem. I think the discouragement of personal excellence, of personal creativity and of personal enterprise begins with the religion. Islam itself holds back its own followers from great creative achievements. Let us look at how this happens as we continue to look at the performance factor.

The origin of the problem of lack of performance within the Moslem world is the way that any creativity is viewed, even in children. I am using the word creativity here to signify an action considered outside of the mainstream. When a child expresses a thought, through speech, or drawing a picture, or in their play, it can often be creative. The problem in the Islamic culture is that when this happens, if the activity doesn't conform to Islamic norms then the child is discouraged from pursuing it. If the child continues in the creative activity, punishment comes. Basically it is beaten out of the child as a way of ensuring submission to Islam at an early age. The child learns to conform or at least keep ideas to him or herself. The attitude of "conform to Islam" is pushed into the Soul through the gateway of the Will, and it is accompanied with, "if you don't there will be severe negative consequences."

At the individual level, this "conform to Islam" attitude is received as discouragement to step outside of acceptable social boundaries. Now, I believe that boundaries are very healthy for us, but these boundaries are imposed on people from outside of the Soul and not developed internally by a person. This means that the boundaries are necessarily constraining and restrictive, to support Islamic perspectives. The overall effect of this squashing of creativity, of this punishing of asking questions, and of forced submission to Islam is an under-performing culture. Probably there is nowhere where this is more evident than in the world of sports. There are about 1.2 billion Moslems in the world, nearly 20 % of the population of the world. Do they hold close to 20 % of world records, or get about 20% of the world's medals in international sports? In case you didn't know, the answer is emphatically no!

In Chapter 8 we looked at performance and showed how a drive to perform can lead a person to get on their own personal "Hamster Wheel" in their life. This is a rare event in the Islamic world, as any fire in the belly to do things is doused with the sour water of Islamic conformance. If the practitioners of Islam don't change their ways in this matter, they will continue to under-perform, and keep their people in systemized poverty. I can't help feeling a great sense of sadness for the people in this situation. There is so much talent in the Moslem world that goes to waste, and we are all poorer because of it.

It is now time to look at Acceptance, the "A" of SPAR, within the religion of Islam. The issue here is, 'How do I feel about myself, due to what others think and feel about me?" I see this as a two-part problem in

26

the world of Islam, namely acceptance of and from other people and acceptance of and from their god, Allah.

Acceptance within Islam, or put another way, acceptance between Moslems, is related to the conformity we discussed earlier. Simply put, if self-imposed conformity to whatever sect of Islam within their immediate social group is present, a person is more likely to feel accepted. I think there is a need to go back into a little history here. When Islam was being formed in the deserts of what we now call Saudi Arabia, the culture was a tribal culture. It was the social method chosen by what we call the Arabs, which was the most proficient for survival. So at its core, acceptance back then meant survival in the desert, as rejection could mean almost certain death. Islam changed things some, but the characteristic nature, that of tribal acceptance, stayed in its importance. Even though the modern world seems to be slowly influencing this important social truth and changing it, the tribal lines still seem to exist. These lines between tribes, which can be thought of as big extended families, are easy to picture as lines of acceptance.

For the individual Moslem then, acceptance is a significant thing. There are two social pressures that drive the need to feel accepted, conformity to Islam, and tribal divides. In fact, when we look at the birth of Islam, we can see this at work. Mohammed, their prophet, and his message, were rejected by the townspeople (tribe) in Mecca, where he lived. So he went to the neighboring town of Medina, where some of the people there accepted Mohammed and his message. Eventually, the whole of Medina converted to this new religion, accepting Mohammed, and went with him and conquered Mecca, and forced conversion of the Meccan people to Islam. In my opinion, Mohammed was so driven by his need to be accepted that he was willing to kill those who didn't accept him, even from his own family group and tribe. Of course, like all good religious fanatics, he hid his personal need for acceptance, and did it behind the message of Allah, his god. Even now, if one criticizes Islam or Mohammed it can result in a violent outcome, and acceptance is the issue.

I could probably write a whole book about this one subject, but I won't. I hope that you have gotten an understanding of how acceptance is a major emotional factor within the religion of Islam.

At the individual level, acceptance and its opposite, rejection, is a major factor in interpersonal relationships for the Moslem. Their whole outlook and worldview is dominated by this factor. The roots of the power of acceptance in Moslems goes to the belief system of Islam, and ancient tribal pressures involving the survival of the individual and the family group. The power of acceptance in the life of a Moslem will cause him or her to do things that help to gain or maintain that acceptance. Such irrational behavior as suicide bombings, demonstrating over cartoons, and honor killings are all related to acceptance at a personal level. Not only is the emotional prison of Islam real, it is dangerous as it threatens the life of any individuals who become objects of wrath.

I have not really talked much about the subject of acceptance from the god of the Moslems, Allah. I think that this needs to be included in what I am about to discuss, the "R" in SPAR, Responsibility.

The problem of personal responsibility for Moslems is great. If you recall it revolves around the question, "How do I feel about myself, due to my ability to meet certain standards?" At the beginning of this section of the book, which covers Islam, I made a statement that I thought the religion was dysfunctional. I further said that I found the Koran to be a chaotic book. It is within this "responsibility" factor that it is easiest to see.

Within the Koran and Hadith, the two pieces of written literature relied on most heavily by Moslems for guidance in how to conduct life, there are considerable inconsistencies. Since this "R" factor is all about trying to meet certain standards, the inconsistencies can be a problem. Let me give you a couple of examples. The Koran says that Allah gave the Jews and Christians the "Taurat" and "Injeel", meaning the Torah and Gospel, and yet they, Moslems, are to reject these two books as being flawed, and they are not to read them. This brings up a second problem, how could their perfect god, Allah, create these two books that are imperfect according to the final revelation of the Koran? Moslems are also taught that Isa, the Islamic name for Jesus, is the Son of God, but is not divine, and that he was crucified but didn't die, and so was not resurrected.

If a Moslem really considers these things in a rational sense, a problem arises. The Koran is supposed to be the perfect revelation of Allah, but it has standards of belief that are not based on reason. Either Allah is perfect and always does perfect things or he is not.

There is more! Within Islam there is something called the five pillars. This is a series of five duties that every Moslem is expected to undertake. They are Shahadah (profession of faith), Salah (ritual prayer), Zakah (alms tax), Sawm (fasting during Ramadan), and Hajj (pilgrimage to Mecca). There are other duties that are also undertaken which are not considered as important. The two other major duties are Tawalla (loving the immediate family) and Jihad (Struggle). That last one has become famous in the last few years! Taken as a combined package they are a daunting set of standards to try to keep.

There is one big standard that I alluded to at the end of the discussion about acceptance. Does a Moslem meet Allah's standards, and is he or she accepted? This is a question only the individual Moslem can answer. To me it looks like it would be very easy to fail Allah, and not match up to all the instructions in the Koran.

As we have talked about before, when some people cannot meet the "certain standards" it can result in negative feelings about oneself. This is as true for a Moslem as for anybody. Moslems can be dealing with questions inside their Soul like, "Am I good enough in my prayers, Will I ever be able to go on the Hajj and have I done Jihad to Allah's satisfaction?" The inability to meet the standards will result in feelings like hopelessness, inadequacy or shame.

Islam Is the Prison

I have spent a considerable amount of time on the subject of Islam as it relates to emotional prisons, and I believe it is justified because of the effects of it as a religion. We have seen through doing the SPAR analysis how each of these four factors is at work in the lives of Moslems. At an individual level any one of these factors can result in a person getting trapped, and Moslems face the distinct possibility of having to deal with all four. The religion of Islam is one of the most dangerous prisons that exists in the world. It is a religion of power and control, and it convinces its adherents that performing immoral acts like lying, cheating, and stealing is acceptable. It can even induce the ability of its followers to engage in some evil behaviors, such as murdering innocent people, while being convinced that they are doing good. All this happens in the name of Allah.

Islam is an emotional prison, holding the Souls of Moslems.

Judaism

Just in case there are people that don't know it, Judaism and Christianity follow and worship the same God. The religions have much in common, having the same basic religious book, which the Judaists might call the Law and the Prophets, and Christians call the Old Testament. Christians however also have the New Testament, which they believe is the further revelation of God beyond the Old Testament. The point of difference is simple. Christians believe that Jesus is the Messiah prophesied or foretold in the Old Testament, and Judaists don't.

I pondered where to start looking at this religion, and I came to a point where I had to begin by identifying the "whom" of Judaism and not the "what." Judaism is practiced by Jews, and Jews are said to be God's chosen people. This very phrase "chosen people" is part of the problem that Jews have in the context of emotional prisons. Let us see what God actually said to them about being "chosen."

Dt 7:6 - For you are a holy people to the Lord your God; the Lord your God has chosen you to be a people for His own possession out of all the peoples who are on the face of the earth.

While there is a tremendous amount that can be said about this verse, there are a couple of important points I want to cover for our discussion. First, Jews are "chosen." When a person believes they are chosen it can often result in feelings of superiority, leading to the unfortunate problem of pride. The second point is that the phrase "out of all the peoples" reinforces this sense of superiority when it is interpreted as being above everybody else, making the pride problem worse.

Just for the record let's state what the "chosen, out of all people means." God promised Abraham, often called the father of the Jews, that He, God, would bless him. This blessing would come in the form of descendents who would become a great nation, and bless all the families of the world. (This promise is found in Genesis 12:2-3) So the descendents of Abraham, the Jews, were chosen to bless the entire world. When you take this word "chosen" and look at the entire Bible, you get a different picture of what God meant. He first meant that the Jews were chosen to carry the word of God to the whole world. More than that though they were chosen as the people group to whom the Messiah, who is the Savior of the world, would be born to. Christians maintain that Jesus is that Messiah, and He is called the Word of God in the New

30

Testament. Being chosen is not about being above others, it is being chosen to fulfill part of God's plan for humanity, that is, being selected to bring us all the word of God.

Let us take a look at some of the characteristics of Judaism that point the Jewish people into dysfunctional and compulsive behaviors. The big one to me is the immense amount of legalism. What I mean by legalism is the constant strict adherence to the Law. For Jews this begins with the Ten Commandments and the other laws given to the Jewish people. But Jewish religious leaders over the years have added to these laws, to such a point that it is almost impossible to keep them all. Let us see what this does in the Soul of a person.

First a person becomes aware, usually as a young child, that "law" exists, and it is seen as a set of rules and regulations to live by, and it is a matter of obedience to God. In the Mind (where knowledge, understanding and wisdom reside), they have acquired the knowledge of the law, but usually do not understand its meaning and purpose. As a person's Soul begins to develop and mature, greater understanding of the "Law" comes, and with it wisdom begins to be acquired.

Next comes the response to the "Law" and all it means, and this is where trouble may begin. A person can start to accept the "Law" into his or her Heart and develop values around the "Law", beliefs in the "Law", and attitudes about the "Law." Simply put, the "Law" becomes anywhere on a spectrum from highly important to completely ignored. At the high importance end, a person tends to become highly religious, absorbed in all the nitty gritty details, and tries hard to be compliant with it. At the completely ignored end a person rejects religion, doesn't care about rules and pleases themselves in their activities. In both cases it is due to the guilt inducing capability of the "Law" or at least trying to keep it.

Let me explain this thing I have called "guilt inducing capability." A set of rules and regulations like the "Law" has a normal Soul response that goes with it. If the "Law" is broken by an individual, then the process I described in an earlier chapter on how an emotion develops takes place. The emotion that is generated within the Soul is guilt. When we do something that we know is wrong, we feel guilty, and that is the "designed in" response. In a court of law, we plead guilty or not guilty to a charge that we have broken some law. This sort of general response to rules and regulations is of course not exclusive to the Jews, and any social group can find themselves in it. What is a problem is the unique situation that the Jews are in.

The unique situation is that from their very formation as a people group, they have been subject to the "Law." They were the first to receive it and it came directly from God. It was part of God's plan for them, the Jews, in remaining separate as a chosen people. So, from the very beginning of their existence, they have become very aware of the problem of guilt in their lives, and it has become a characteristic of their social identity.

What does this guilt do to individuals who are Jewish? For the people who take the "Law" very seriously, they carry a burden around at all times, the burden of actual and real guilt. They know and understand that every human being has broken the "Law", and may even do so daily. Within themselves they may strive to constantly do better to keep the "Law", believing that each day they are becoming closer to what God wants them to be. This is a "hamster wheel" approach to life. Culturally, meaning it is part of the Jewish social fabric, this can actually produce great accomplishments, which might account for the high level of success Jewish people have in life.

Some Jews feeling the burden of guilt may choose to respond to it in a different way. They may choose to accept the guilt as just the way things are, and try to live out life acknowledging it but not letting it run their day-to-day activities. Others may respond by trying to remove the guilt or suppress it by rejecting the "Law." After all isn't the "Law" the source of guilt? Ultimately though, for a Jew, rejection of the "Law" is a rejection of God.

Let us summarize this set of thoughts. The Jews were the receivers of the "Law" from God, and were told to keep it. Guilt is the normal response to breaking the "Law", and from the beginning of their existence the Jews have carried guilt as individuals and as a culture. The individual response to this guilt ranges from working harder to keep the "Law", to accepting the guilt, but moving through life not paying much attention to it. A further response to this guilt is the rejection of the "Law", and rejection of God. Now we can look at Judaism through our SPAR method.

For the first SPAR factor, Security, I would give Jews a high mark. As individuals I have not found them to have a sense of insecurity. In this

32

factor we look at the question, "How do I feel about myself?" I really think that Jews feel very comfortable and secure. In my opinion this is also cultural, just like the guilt characteristic, and comes as a result of the belief that they are chosen. The reason for being chosen may be lost for a lot of Jews, but the underlying sense of being special and more important than others still remains. The downside of this is that some Jewish people seem to have an air of pride or arrogance, and others have a sense of entitlement.

The next SPAR factor is "P" for performance. Our question here is, "How do I feel about myself, due to the things I do?" The cultural characteristic of guilt I have described means that some Jewish individuals will struggle with this, both consciously and unconsciously. Some will be driven to higher and higher levels of performance, others will give up realizing that they can never achieve perfection. There also seems to be a link between the characteristics of God described in the Jewish scriptures about His "excellence" and the attitude of the Jewish people about themselves. He is described as being able to perform great deeds and Jews, in a cultural sense, think that they can also perform great things. This can lead to great achievements but also great disaster.

I know that a lot of readers might be saying, what is he, (that is me as the writer), talking about? You might even disagree with this whole discussion of the "performance" of Jews. My answer to this is to look at how Jews actually perform in the world. I am going to point out a few things to demonstrate how this focus on performance has played itself out.

On the negative end of this performance attitude is the constant turning away from their traditional values, as enshrined in the "Law." This could be thought of as rejection of these values, or disobedience to the law, or rebellion! God Himself, in the Jewish scriptures, calls them "stiff-necked" people. Let us see what being stiff-necked did to them!

The Jewish people constantly turned away from God. In fact there is a complete book that describes this, the book of Judges. The worst case of this though, in my opinion, is found at the time of King Ahaz. Led by the king, the nation of the Jews turned away from God and worshipped a false god called Baal. One of the results was the sacrifice of live children who were thrown into the fire; Ahaz even put one of his own infant children to death in it. What kind of Soul gets to believe that it is a wise thing to do, sacrificing one's own child? It is a Soul of a person who believes that by performing the act of child sacrifice, life will be better in some way.

My second example is that of the rejection of Jesus as the Messiah by the Jews. Here was a man, Jesus, who fulfilled all the prophecies that the Jews had about who the Messiah would be, and they killed Him! The high priest of the Jews at the time, Caiaphas, decided that it was best to have Jesus killed. The reasoning of Caiaphas was that the Romans, who ruled the Jews at the time, wouldn't take the whole nation away. The book of John, Chapter 11, verses 47 to 53, details this. Notice that again a human sacrifice was to be made! This was another example of doing something, performing, that made the perpetrator feel better about themselves. This whole subject of the reasons for Jesus being murdered is a fascinating study for those that may be interested, but I won't cover it here as it is outside the scope of the book.

My third example of how performance has been a problem is the Holocaust. It is traditional to blame Hitler, the Nazis and the German people for the killing of as many as six million Jews. I have to agree that they are a big part of the problem, however the Jews themselves have a part in it. From the very beginning Hitler, the German leader, had said he was going to get rid of the "Jewish problem." The Jews chose to either not believe or ignore him and what he was planning. When it was apparent that they were in physical jeopardy, did they remove themselves from harm? No, they believed they could handle it, they thought they were able to overcome it; they were going to perform their way out of the problem. Once they finally realized that this problem wasn't going to be overcome, they slipped into hopelessness. This was another manifestation of performance; somehow they were guilty of doing something and deserved this treatment.

I am going to say, that I have had to approach all three of my examples from a simplistic perspective, I have been merely trying to show how performance was part of the problem. I would ask the reader to see something, all three of my examples revolve around the killing of innocent people.

Moving to the positive side we can see that the drive to perform can indeed bring great things. The first example is what I'm going to call, "life from the desert." Prior to the creation of current Jewish state, the land we now call Israel was a wasteland, dry, barren and unproductive. It had been completely mismanaged by the previous inhabitants. The

Jewish people have transformed it through their efforts to such a point that rainfall has increased, crop production is sufficient enough to feed the nation and it is green again. This is a very good example of performance at work.

The second positive example is the Jewish military. I know that this could be a strange example to consider, but bear with me. Since the beginning of the current state of Israel they have been under a constant threat of attack from every direction possible. Each time they have been challenged by stronger and more numerous military forces they have succeeded in repelling the aggressors and have actually captured land. I believe part of the reason for this is that the performance orientation of each person making up the military contributes to its success.

The last example is a very interesting one. When one looks at all the winners of Nobel prizes, an amazing number of them are Jewish. When I totaled the number of prizes for achievement won by people of Jewish heritage I was amazed. I excluded the prize for peace, as this seems to be a political prize not an actual achievement award. Did you know that out of a possible 684 prizes, 167 have gone to Jewish winners. That is 24.4%! Less than 1% of the world population is Jewish, and they won over 24% of the most prestigious achievement award available. In case you might think this is a fluke, there is more. Jewish people have won 38% of the US National Science Awards ever given out. Performance at work!

I have spent a lot of time and space on this performance subject because it deserves it. The very nature of a performance-obsessed personality is one of being driven by emotions. Properly harnessed it can lead to very good outcomes, but unrestrained it can be devastating. For Jews this is true as a people group and as individuals. The downside is an emotional trap, which can often lead to other emotional prisons like perfectionism or victimhood.

The next SPAR factor is "A" for Acceptance. I don't find this to be as big an issue as it is for other groups. Having a cultural sense of being chosen means you have a sense of being accepted. Individual Jews may struggle with this issue, but I don't believe the religion itself promotes any feelings of rejection in its followers.

The last SPAR factor is "R" for responsibility, where we ask ourselves the question, "How do I feel about myself due to my ability to meet certain standards?" The answer here is "guilty." I covered this issue earlier when I discussed the amount of legalism that is built into the Jewish national identity or culture. The response by an individual to this cultural sense of feeling guilty will of course differ from person to person. Some will strive harder to meet certain standards, which is one way to deal with the negative emotion of guilt. Others will slip into further negative feeling states like despair or shame. In some of these cases the individual might choose to deal with these powerful feelings by some form of self-medication like alcohol, drugs or pornography. We have seen before that these are emotional prisons.

From the perspective of this book and its subject of emotional prisons, the question of what Judaism does to its adherents has been challenging. We have seen that following this religion leads to a cultural sense of guilt though its very legalistic practices. This guilt dominates the Soul responses of every Jewish believer to life in one way or another. For some it becomes a driver for success, for others it leads into some form of emotional trap. Judaism, as practiced, is an emotional prison.

Next we will take an in-depth look at how Christianity can be an emotional prison or lead others into one through some of its dysfunctions.

14

CHRISTIANITY

I like your Christ; I do not like your Christians. Your Christians are so unlike your Christ.
Mahatma Gandhi

I must begin this look at Christianity and emotional prisons by stating that I am a Christian. Christianity is my religion, and I would probably be categorized as an evangelical Christian who lives on the "religious right." I believe in the essentials of the Christian faith that are; salvation by grace alone, Jesus' atonement for my sins, Jesus' bodily resurrection from the dead, Christ is both man and God, and the Trinity (God as three persons). Other doctrines that I consider essential and believe; the Virgin Birth, inerrancy of Scripture, sin and its consequences, that angels exist, the Second Coming of Christ, the Church as the Bride of Christ, the existence of Satan and his followers, and the existence of hell. I say all this to be clear, theologically speaking, to anyone who reads what I am about to write about.

Being a Christian does not protect you from falling into an emotional prison. In this issue a Christian is no different to any other religious person! Some Christians will reject that message or find it hard to accept. Psychologists call this denial, I call it dishonest. If you are a Christian reading this, and have the errant view that everything is better because you are a Christian, please wake up. Let me illustrate this truth with a famous verse of Scripture found in the book of Romans, Chapter 3, verse 23:

For all have sinned and fall short of the glory of God.

Notice the word "**all**" this means every person. No one is exempt! This fact will be true for all of us until we physically die. Deep down, every emotional prison has a root of sin. Some of us are able to deal with the issue of sins better than others, (I have not been one of them!), and others have not dealt with this well. It is the people that don't deal with sin well and get overcome with their own emotions who get trapped. Christians are not exempt!

There is though, a big difference between Christians and all other people; it is that we have the hope of healing because of whom we believe in. I will be covering this subject in detail later in the third book. Let us now look at some of the dysfunctions within Christianity that help push people into emotional prisons.

In my opinion the biggest single factor in getting Christians trapped in emotional prisons and keeping them there is "denial." I'm going to look at several areas of denial in modern day Christianity. They are:

- Denial of the Truth
- Denial of Doctrine
- Denial of Faith
- Denial of Grace
- Denial of Application

Denial of the Truth

This is the denial that Jesus is the embodiment of truth. It is one thing for a non-Christian to say that Jesus is not the truth, and He doesn't "save" anybody, but it is awful to hear people who call themselves Christians deny it. This denial happens in many ways. There is outright denial and there is partial denial. When a person has heard about Jesus and yet fully denies that He is the truth, they are simply not a Christian, and if they go to church it is probably for reasons other than spiritual growth.

It is the partial deniers who are church leaders that irritate me. What good is the Bible if it contains things that are not truth? That makes it a book of lies! Within Christianity there are people who are leading and teaching others who have read the Scriptures, and still deny some things about Jesus. Perhaps the worst group of so-called leaders is the "Jesus Seminar." Let us look at what they do and say.

First let me be sure to let you know that the "Jesus Seminar" has a website and publishes books and magazines. I recommend that you do not poison your Mind or your Heart by reading any of their material. The way they approach their work is couched in "scholarly terms" like this; "We are searching for the historical Jesus." Sounds good, doesn't it? What they actually do is to deny, by questioning, that Jesus was born of a virgin. Some of the members even deny He was resurrected. They deny that He said all the things laid out in the Gospels, and they deny that He performed the miracles attributed to Him. Maybe worst of all, some of them even deny the deity of Christ.

Now for a warning! When you see a TV program about Christianity, beware. Some of the so-called scholars the journalists look to for answers belong to this group. They are being given complete access to our Souls as Christians and are able to plant unrefuted doubts in our Hearts and the Hearts of our children. I'm all for scholarly questioning, but these types of people deny facts to come to their conclusions, and then insist they are telling the truth.

The denial of who Jesus is, which is the Truth, has serious implications. If we cannot rely on the fact that Jesus is the Truth, then the whole foundation of our faith erodes, and nothing matters. It is a spiritual recipe; mix up some truth with some lies, and bake in the Mind of an unsuspecting person and you get a Soul of confusion. How does a badly confused Soul deal with life? They jump into actions that help ease the confusion; they head off to emotional prisons.

When a person is in confusion about what is true about another person or what he or she says, their ability to trust that person is at best diminished, and more than likely disappears. This is accurate for a Christian who gets confused about the truth of Jesus, who He was and what He said. This confusion leads from mistrust to disbelief and sometimes even complete rejection by a person. For a Christian who finds themselves in this position this means that they lose their spiritual mooring. The loss of spiritual mooring adds to the confusion and makes it harder to deal with the normal problems of life that bring other negative emotions with them, like guilt and shame. Ultimately all this confusion and negativity leads to emotional pain as an individual struggles with things. As we have seen before, this can lead to any of us turning to a behavior of self-medicating which can put us into an emotional prison.

Denial of Doctrine

This is similar in nature to the previous discussion on the denial of truth, but is less about Jesus as "the Truth" and more about the things that are presented as truths in the Scriptures. When thinking about this dysfunction within the Christian world I focus on what I called earlier "the essentials." So let us look at some of the denials of doctrine that we can see in some parts of what the public thinks of as "Christianity."

There are some "Christians" who do not believe in the trinity as laid out in the Bible, this is best exemplified by "Oneness Pentecostals." One of the other errors found in the Pentecostal movement is the denial of the doctrine of salvation by grace alone. There are others who do not believe that Jesus is God, the most prominent of these would be the Jehovah's Witnesses. These are cults, because they deny the truth of Scripture and they also have some common characteristics.

They were all founded by individuals who claim that they received some special revelation from God. They all rewrite the Bible to match this new revelation. They all persuade some early followers that they are "right", and that their rightness is not to be questioned. They all use intense indoctrination techniques to persuade someone to join them. They all brainwash their followers. They all use fear, guilt and shame to keep their followers coming back. Their leaders all exercise power and control over their congregants to maintain their position and sometimes a lavish lifestyle.

As you might imagine, they really can mess people up! A great example of this would be the followers of James Jones who founded the "Peoples Temple." In 1978 they committed mass suicide; over 900 people died. The point here is that denial of doctrines laid out in Scripture can lead to becoming trapped, and in the extreme, death. People trapped in these movements are convinced that they are "right." Their values, beliefs and attitudes lead them into a life containing fear, guilt and shame, some of the more important precursors to emotional prisons. The individuals trapped in these cults cannot see this, and would deny that they are trapped. It is only when they get out and somehow get deprogrammed that they can admit these things.

There are other less damaging, although still problematical, denials of doctrines that occur within what we might call the mainline church. Things like denial of the virgin birth, or conception through the Holy Spirit. It could also be the denial of the inerrancy of Scripture, or that Satan and his followers are still at work, or maybe the deniers say that hell is a mythical place. While these things are probably not going to stop someone from becoming a Christian, they are foot in the door problems.

A "foot in the door problem" refers back to the old days of door-to-door salesmen. When the salesmen would put his or her foot in the doorway to stop you, the potential buyer, from closing it. Then they would proceed to try to sell you something, let us say it was a vacuum cleaner. If you bought it they would then try to sell you the accessories, bags and cleaning agents. Then they might come back later to sell you some disposable items.

So it is with the deniers. First they sell an idea, which is an error or deviancy from the truth, they have their foot in the door of your Heart. The denier is placing incorrect ideas through the gateway of your Will and if you are not careful, you will believe them. This is the core problem; it leads you to believe that the Scriptures are not fully true. Beyond that you start to believe that God is not telling you the truth, and that He is not everything He says He is. This can further degrade into not believing that He is in control, and will work everything out in the end. The ultimate place one might end up is the emotional prison of hopelessness. This is because if you start to turn doubts and questions into unbelief, nothing is true, and the negative feelings of having no hope eventually arrive in your Soul.

Denial of Faith

The book of Hebrews gives us the Scriptural view or definition of faith in Chapter 11, verse 1:

Now faith is the assurance of things hoped for, the conviction of things not seen.

While I have used the term "denial" it might also be called twisting of faith. That is because some in the Christian world take this verse and basically say, "If you hope for it, it will come to pass." This is a perversion of faith as described in Scripture, but I will let others who are more theologically capable than me explain it (see the bibliography).

I am more concerned with what this error does to people. Think of all the faith challenges that we hear. Let me list three that are common:

- Healing through faith
- Prosperity through faith
- Victory though faith

The error message often delivered here is, "if you had enough faith, you would be healed or become wealthy or be able to overcome adversity."

41

Now I know that some well-meaning people often say things like that - the problem is sometimes sincere sounding self-serving people say it too! The first kind are motivated by trying to help others, and though being in error is unfortunate because it is damaging, I cannot judge them for it. The second kind of person does it intentionally, and can be motivated by a desire for power over others, fame or money. I do judge these, and I want to tell you why.

Let us suppose that you go to an incorrectly motivated faith healer. They do whatever they do, but you are not healed of your condition. What happens? First, it seems that faith has failed. From the faith healers perspective, this failure needs to be removed from the scene, that means you. Second, the faith healer will almost inevitably blame you as not having enough faith, or maybe having some secret thing in your life, which is a barrier to healing. Third and last, your faith will be weakened, due to the failure, and you might even think God has deserted you.

So I do judge that self-serving individual who deceives us in our beliefs and then abandons us, blames us or weakens our faith. Let us also remember that he or she is doing this over and over again to people who are hurting or desperate for relief from pain or poverty or oppression.

What happens in the Soul of a person who goes through such a process? They begin by opening up the gateway of their Will, out of hope, to the message of the faith healer. They pray, they pay and they wait. When nothing changes, negative emotions begin to appear, and questions arise. Doesn't God love me? Where is my healing? Why have I been abandoned? Don't I have enough faith? Do I have some secret dark thing lurking in my Soul? The end point of all of this is a loss or a severe damaging of faith. Some people when faced with this situation will turn to some compulsion to ease the new emotional pain that has entered their life. They have started to head toward an emotional prison, and they are worse off than they were before they went.

This whole analytical process can be repeated for any area where you hear the general message that goes something like this. "Pray in faith for what you want and God will give it to you." Think about it; when a preacher says pray for that new job and you will get it for sure, and it doesn't come, how are you going to feel? The proponents of this kind of theology always have an out, and they weaken the Christian world.

Now I do want to make sure to state that there are some legitimate spiritual victories won through praying and believing out of faith. There are some individuals who are very responsible in their work of helping people through their problems with health, poverty or oppression. I firmly believe that God is still in the business of Soul healing. It is the deniers and deceivers who misinterpret and misuse the faith of the Bible I am concerned about.

Denial of Grace

I like to think of grace as the oil of Christianity. Love is the engine that gives us the power to live our lives, to grow, to move forward and to overcome trials. Grace is what keeps it all running smoothly. Grace has been called "unmerited favor", a definition I like. It flows like heavenly oil into our lives and we are to spread it around to keep our lives moving smoothly.

There are some people, though, who like to receive the grace, and not pass it on; these are the deniers of grace. The greatest need of any person that ever existed, or will exist, is to be saved from the consequences of their sin. There is a scripture that tells us how to become "saved":

Eph 2:8-9 - For by grace you have been saved through faith; and that not of yourselves, it is the gift of God; not as a result of works, so that no one may boast.

It is a mystery to me that seemingly intelligent people cannot grasp the simple truth that grace is a gift of God, and it is a gift that keeps on giving, and the more we give it away the more we get from God.

Why do so many Christians, including those called to preach the word of God, not live a life full of grace? Why do they deny others around them the truth of the power of grace? Why is unforgiveness, a withholding of grace, so prevalent in the Christian community? Why do so many denominations believe that their way is the best or even the only way to get saved? I can hardly believe this, but there are some Christians who believe a person has to be baptized to be saved. This is a complete denial of grace.

The answers to these questions lie in the natural selfishness of men. Denying grace to others is an attempt to control them for self-serving reasons. Unforgiveness, a denial of grace, is a method of trying to keep

43

the offending party in a state of guilt. Not accepting others the way they are is another denial of grace, and it is as about an ungodly a choice as a person can make.

From the perspective of our book topic, denying grace has several implications. An important implication is that it can lead to loneliness through the systematic destruction of relationships. Loneliness is an emotional state that can result in a person "acting out" particularly in some form of love addiction. A second consequence could be that a person who has no grace given to them feels unworthy, another emotional condition that can lead to "acting out."

A third major consequence, and the most important, is that when we deny grace, we can slip into the thinking that we need to work our way into heaven. This is very problematical because we all recognize work is virtuous activity. Christianity is the only religion that says that you cannot earn your way into paradise. One of the reasons is of course that God knows that we tend to get trapped, emotionally speaking, by work. We get on the "hamster wheel" I spoke of in earlier chapters. He, God, also knows that we can become slaves to religious leaders who persuade us to do things to earn salvation. Finally, let me simply pose this question; how can we do enough work to make it into heaven? We cannot, and that is why we need God's grace.

By far and away the most well known Christian song is the old hymn, "Amazing Grace." There is a reason for this; it is because grace is amazing! Let us all resolve to be givers of grace as well as receivers, and to not be deniers. In fact, we ought to look for opportunities to give all the grace we have inside our Hearts away, because God will fill up our engine with more, He will never let us run dry.

Denial of Application

What do you think that might mean? I get this from the following scripture found in the book of Matthew, Chapter 28, verses 18 to 20; this is often referred to as the great commission:

And Jesus came up and spoke to them, saying, "All authority has been given to Me in heaven and on earth. Go therefore and make disciples of all the nations, baptizing them in the name of the Father and the Son and the Holy Spirit, teaching them to observe all that I commanded you; and lo, I am with you always, even to the end of the age. "

It is verse 20 which says to "teach them to observe all I have commanded you" which is important to us here. The original disciples were instructed to teach us, as new disciples, to observe what Jesus has commanded. Simply put, we are to obey Christ and apply His teachings in our lives. However, there are some among us who deny we are to do this; these are the "deniers of application."

To a certain extent I think all Christians "deny application" in their lives. I am not going to say that this is acceptable, but it is understandable. We, and I count myself among this group, are all WIPs, works in progress. The issue for me is not that we don't meet the standard set by Christ; it is that we are actively working toward that standard. What bothers me are the people that say we don't have to do this, the deniers.

In the New Testament there are over 50 commands to do something to or for "one another." They cover all kinds of subjects; we are to accept, love, honor, respect, encourage, affirm and so on. Some of us think we don't have to do those things, and we are wrong. Let me give you one example of this. God gives us a simple command to follow within a marriage, which is found in Ephesians, Chapter 5 verse 33, and it says:

Nevertheless, each individual among you also is to love his own wife even as himself, and the wife must see to it that she respects her husband.

Simple, right? The man is to love his wife, and the woman is to respect her husband. How many Christian marriages actually follow these two commands? (There is a terrific book about this issue, see the bibliography) Are you a denier on this one issue?

I don't want to belabor the subject, because I could probably write another book on it. I only want to go to the bottom line on it. When we don't do things Christ's way, we live less fulfilling lives than are possible. We cling to doing things our own way, which could be called insane! It is actually a form of arrogance, thinking that our way is better than God's.

The problem with being a "denier of application" is that we are actually guilty, and in our Minds we know that, and in our Hearts we realize our attitudes are wrong. Negative feelings can arise from just this factor alone. When we add in feelings of guilt, shame or inadequacy that come up as we live a life of disrespect or unforgiveness or some other disobedient action, the pot gets full, and we often choose to "act out" in some way.

It may not be a familiar thought to you, but here it is. Not obeying Christ's commands may not keep you out of heaven, but your choice of disobedience can sure make your life miserable, and put you into an emotional prison while on the earth.

Shooting the Wounded

One of the great disappointments I have in the way Christianity is practiced is this "shooting the wounded" thing we do. This term, "shooting the wounded" goes back to ancient times, where it was originally "killing the wounded" and referred to what would happen after a battle. There were two sides in a fight, the good guys and the bad guys. When the good guys won they would then finish off their victory in the field by killing any of the opposition who were left wounded. They would also kill off their own wounded if they believed that they wouldn't make it, which might be thought of as a form of mercy. It all sounds callous, but that is what they did. It actually still happens today, although we might label it "ethnic cleansing", or "gang warfare."

Christians do this! We sometimes think of ourselves as the "good guys" and everybody else are the "bad guys." Although we may not be in an actual physical battle, we still have a mindset of them versus us. We might call it a culture war, or even a clash of worldviews, but it is still perceived by us as a fight. In fact, the Apostle Paul warned us about this error of thinking in the book of Ephesians:

Eph 6:12 - For our struggle is not against flesh and blood,

Let us look at what we actually do as we go about our daily lives as Christians, remembering we are talking about "shooting the wounded" and in the context of emotional prisons.

First I want to look at how some of us deal with non-Christians. When a non-believer gets into bad behaviors, addictions or some other form of Soul troubles, what do we do? Some of us are actually pleased or even delighted that the "bad guys" are receiving the consequences of their

46

actions and choices. Think about your own reaction to hearing the news that a Hollywood celebrity has been picked up on a DUI, or a politician has been caught taking a bribe, or when a TV evangelist (who may be a believer) is discovered to be using a prostitute. Do you take worldly joy in the news, are you secretly pleased that one of the "high and mighty" has fallen? I confess that I have done that in the past. Well, these people are wounded.

Let us now bring this down to our own neighborhood. Do we delight when that grouchy old drunk down the street has something go wrong? Are we pleased when we hear that two "gang-bangers" kill one another? Do we want revenge when our next-door neighbor hits our dog in the street with his car, when he might have avoided it?

Do we want to punish these people more? Don't we feel like the consequences of their actions aren't severe enough? Of course we do, we want to shoot the wounded. Scripture is very clear on this subject, that if we want to do something bad to somebody, particularly out of anger, it is as if we had already done it. This is, of course, a problem of the Soul. Wanting revenge, or desiring to punish another person are emotional responses that can cause us to act out. Acting out, as we have seen before is part of the process of becoming trapped into an emotional prison.

Most of us don't go as far as acting out against non-believers who are wounded people and that we might perceive as having hurt us in some way. We do shoot them though, but in a more subtle way. We disassociate ourselves from them, perhaps ignoring them. We take them to court and sue. We gossip and slander them. We crack jokes about them. We slip into the human seat of judgment. All the time we do this we ignore the fact that these are hurting people too. What we typically don't do is to love them more, pray for them and their situation or deal with them as Jesus has shown us to.

Jesus warned us that we were to not be judgmental, to not seek revenge, to not seek retribution, to not shoot the wounded. He gave us what we call the "golden rule", to "do unto others as we would have them do unto us." We Christians are simply not very good about how we treat non-believers who are wounded. We prefer to shoot them instead of recognizing, as Jesus did, that they are hurt people who need loving. Is it any wonder that the world perceives evangelical Christians as "judgmental", because that is what they see, that is how we project ourselves? I will address this a little more a few paragraphs later.

Now let us go to the question of how we treat our own wounded. If anything can be said here it is that we are worse with our own. What do we do when a fellow church member gets into some form of acting out? We reject them! Not maybe in the sense of throwing them out, but we stop talking with them, we ignore them, we gossip about them, we take sides in disputes, we avoid them and we set up a situation where they feel unwelcome. Then when they leave, we feel better, because we don't have to do all those things any more. If you have done any of those things you have basically abused them, and because it is done in a spiritual setting, we ought to call it spiritual abuse. Even as I write this I feel convicted, I hope you do too!

If, as a Christian who is reading this, you sense that I am being hard or even judgmental about how Christians treat each other, it is because I am. I am trying not to be judgmental, but I do want to be pointed about this great moral failure that exists in our churches. This stuff, the stuff that drives people away was done to me, so I am sensitive about it. I can see why the world looks at Christians and calls them a judgmental group.

I mentioned earlier that we project this image of being judgmental. The world is very aware of what Jesus said about how to treat others, and they see that we are not matching the standard, we are not acting in accordance with our beliefs and we are hypocrites. They see that we often shoot people who are wounded. You might be saying that you personally don't do it, but the problem is that when one Christian person does shoot a wounded person, in the eyes of the world, we are all like that. We therefore have a responsibility to one another to discourage the shooting of any wounded person, and offer grace in its place.

You might be asking, what does this "shooting the wounded" have to do with emotional prisons? Everything; that is the answer. Who do we shoot? We shoot the people who are "acting out", the people who might be headed toward a prison, or the people who are already there.

Consider the non-believer who lives down the street who is discovered to have some problem. Maybe he is trading in kiddie-porn, or she is a closet drunk, or their teenage boys have been dealing drugs. Do you invite them to church? No, you do your best to have nothing to do with them. I don't say that in judgment - it is the way we all are, but is it what we ought to do? Instead of embracing the person in trouble, our wounded neighbor, as Jesus always did, we "shoot them."

How about the Christian brother or sister? What do we do when one of our own has some behavioral problems that get exposed? We shoot them! What if a member of your congregation was discovered to be a pedophile, what would you do? Would you support him or her, would you provide help? No, you would demand that he or she was locked up and that the key was thrown away! How many of us would demand that the church assist him or her in getting treatment. How many of us would visit them in jail. How far would our Christian love go?

In the context of emotional prisons, when we "shoot the wounded", we almost always make it worse for the inmate. We actually become part of the problem, not part of the solution. We would rather be the jailers than the people who "set captives free." This is a confession that we must make as Christians if we are to be honest about ourselves as individuals and as a collective body of God's people. In our Bible we are instructed, "imitate Christ", and He said about Himself that He came to "set the captives free."

I don't say these things to shame or guilt the church community; I say them to try to wake them up! The secular world looks at us and sees people who are not different, who do not act in accordance with their own stated beliefs and who shoot their own wounded. When we misapply our religious instructions to the people around us we are guilty of hypocrisy and judgmentalism. These can actually lead us down the path to our own emotional traps. This means that not only are we not helping others, but we are hurting ourselves.

I probably ought to explain that. When we indulge ourselves in things like hypocritical actions and judgmentalism, we allow pride or arrogance to come into our lives. You know what I mean, it is the "holier than you" attitude that some of us have. This is when we actually become vulnerable to our own compulsions. We start to accept the false belief that we really are better than other people, that we can do no wrong. That is when our own compulsive behavior will kick in. It could be that we start to look at pornography, to see what our immoral neighbor is actually looking at. We might take a little wine to relieve the stress of being the local moral police, and a little wine turns into a bottle a day.

In summary, our practice of "shooting the wounded" is a problematical dysfunction within the Christian world. It actually makes a lot of things worse. For the individual who is trapped by some form of "acting out" it often makes their situation worse. For a Christian it can often result in them leaving the organized church, either being thrown out or leaving voluntarily. The Christians who engage in "shooting the wounded" run the risk in their own lives of doing the opposite of what Scripture says. They also make themselves vulnerable to heading into their own emotional prison.

Stinking Thinking

That phrase 'stinking thinking" is not mine, I don't actually know where it comes from, but it an excellent title for this section of the chapter. "Stinking thinking" refers to the way we, as a group of Christians, sometimes apply Scripture to everyday problems. Stinking thinking leads others or us toward emotional difficulties that can then place us squarely on the path to an emotional prison.

At the core of stinking thinking there is a discipleship problem. No, I am not talking about a lack of teaching of what the Bible actually says; it is something different. It looks to me like we are becoming disciples of the church and not disciples of Christ. This may sound like a small difference, but it is not, and it affects how we see one another, and how we treat one another.

Briefly this is it. Some of us in the Christian world follow what our churches and ministers say and not what Christ said. The result of this is that we propagate teachings which are not what Jesus actually said, and some of these teachings lead to aberrant behavior. Let us look at some examples.

I personally knew a minister who was forced to resign from a Southern Baptist church because of some things he spoke of in a closed confidential session. The deacons held private meetings and decided that it was best if he left, and didn't tell the church body the real reason. This is of course also a case of shooting the wounded, but there is more. It illustrates an issue of following a church and not Christ.

The Southern Baptist churches are governed using paid ministers and a board of deacons. That is the error! The New Testament church clearly says to have elders as well as deacons, and there is a difference between

50

these two types of church leaders. I know that any Southern Baptist reading this will be tempted to defend their form of government, but this cannot be defended. It can be rationalized away by misinterpretation, but it is still an error.

In the case of my Southern Baptist minister friend, the deacons basically threw him out. If a board of elders had existed, this may not have happened. This is because elders, who are selected and appointed by other elders, tend to be less quick to jump to judgmentalism, and more likely to try to reconcile and help the minister. Please note that I am not saying that the elders would have not allowed this awful rejection to happen. I am saying that there were no checks and balances in the power structure of the church, because of "stinking thinking" about how the church was governed.

For the record let us look at what happened next to the rejected minister. He left and went into a tailspin, which is understandable since he had been betrayed and rejected. This ultimately resulted in the breakdown of his marriage, an affair, which is a symptom of someone being in an emotional prison, and finally divorce. The error of the church teaching on governance contributed to this disaster.

I have highlighted the error in church governance within the Southern Baptist church system, but I also want to state for the record that on most things the SBC is very sound. I personally think that they are one of the healthiest Christian groups in the world, and I admire their work.

Roman Catholics have a few problems with stinking thinking too! I have to confess that I didn't know much about Roman Catholicism up until a few years ago. It was then I had my first truly eye-opening experience of some of their practices. Although I recognized several things I would question, I am just going to mention three of them.

I went to a Catholic wedding of a family member expecting a liturgical style ceremony, which is what I was part of. It was touching and different to what I was used to, and I enjoyed it. What I didn't expect were the three errors. One is minor and two were more important. The minor error was all the statues of various people I saw inside the church building. In itself it might seem trivial, but the problem was that these were statues or busts of Mary, mother of Jesus, and various "saints." When I noticed these I was reminded that some Catholics I know had said that they pray to or call upon some saints for various reasons. I don't know whether we could call that "idol worship", which would violate the second commandment, but it would seem to take our eyes away from God directly and place our faith on these dead people.

The first major error (remembering that this is my opinion) was when we took communion. As we were all getting ready to do this I heard and incredible statement, which went something like this. "If you are not Catholic you can't take communion with us." So since I'm not a Catholic, I respected that request. However, I was struck then as to how exclusionary that statement was. It excluded me and all other people who are followers of Jesus, and who are not Catholics. I was not offended, but I was saddened by what crossed my Mind. Jesus would never exclude anybody who wanted to commune with Him and celebrate His death and resurrection. This goes to the issues of being rejected, or feeling inadequate, which we have discussed earlier in the first book.

The second major error I saw deals with the subject of Mary, mother of Jesus. After the marriage ceremony, but before the presentation of the couple to us as the witnessing congregation, the couple was instructed to do something. They were to go over to the statue of Mary and ask for a blessing on their marriage. So that's what happened. They went and kneeled down in front of the statue, and prayed to the Virgin Mary. Since I was so familiar with the various Scriptures that talk to us about praying to the living God, it was a little shocking, because it wasn't biblical. I got to wondering how a priest or a church could let such a thing happen.

I learned that this is referred to as the "veneration of Mary", and is thought of as an act of just less than worship. It sure looked like worship to me though! One of the problems with this is that it provides a way for the priesthood to control the congregations using guilt. "Have you prayed to Mary today?" I suppose that has been said many times by Catholic priests who maybe even unthinkingly spoke it. The veneration of Mary is a good example of stinking thinking; it simply cannot be supported from Scripture, which is the Word of God. From the perspective of our subject of emotional prisons, this relates to the feelings of inadequacy through not being good enough or doing enough.

I have used some examples of stinking thinking from a couple of types of Christian churches and could provide many more, but that would be pointless and overkill. There is no one group that has the perfect way. All churches are run by fallible people and will make mistakes. Some of these mistakes lead church members onto paths that are destructive. Some mistakes set up situations that lead people into feeling negative emotions like shame or inadequacy. Some other mistakes heap condemnation and judgment on individuals, which almost says to someone, "go and self-medicate", something which can often steer us into an emotional prison.

Let us now take a look at Christianity from the SPAR analytical perspective.

SPAR and Christianity

The first SPAR factor is Security, where we ask the question, "How do I feel about myself?" The act of becoming a Christian does not change the sense of insecurity in any way in any person. That will be a challenging statement to some, so let me address it up front. Becoming or being a Christian puts an individual in a position to deal with insecurity, but doesn't actually change it unless the person starts to replace old beliefs with new ones. That is part of becoming healed, which is to be covered in the third book. For now I will offer one example of what Scripture actually says about being secure. It is found in Psalm 8, verse 4:

What is man that You take thought of him, and the son of man that You care for him?

The psalmist, David, is asking a rhetorical question. Knowing that we, all of humanity, are not following the God who created us, he asks, "Why do you care about us?" He, of course, knows that God does care about all of us more deeply than we can imagine. The point here is that we can all experience a higher level of personal security by being a Christian and by following the instructions for life laid out in the Bible and finally by accepting His promises into our Hearts.

Unfortunately, there are some practitioners of Christianity who prey on the insecure. I don't know what their true motivations may be, but I suspect that these false prophets and teachers are in their own emotional traps. It looks to me like they, the proponents of falsehoods, need to create a following and a dependency on themselves in the lives of others. They do this to have a better feeling about themselves, to feel more secure. I think that this issue may also include the other SPAR factors too, but the essence in still a personal insecurity. One of the odd things about these false teachers is that they appear to be strong, self-confident and knowledgeable about what the Scriptures say.

What about us poor guys and gals who are dealing with a sense of personal insecurity? Be assured that the actual teachings of the Bible tell us quite clearly that we are fully and totally loved by God with absolutely no pre-conditions. So how is it that some of us fall into a worse state of insecurity after we finally turn to God? It is all about perception; it is about our ability to see things about ourselves, and it is about the work that God starts doing in our lives. It is really very simple, before we became Christians we were insecure and we couldn't change it, so we buried it. After we choose to give our lives to God, we start to experience the insecurity, we see it anew. I know that this may hard to believe but this is actually part of the work God will do in every person who chooses Him. This is because God wants to draw us to Him, the only true secure place for our Souls to be.

The short-term and temporary problem is that our sense of insecurity goes up and it does not feel good at all! Have you ever wondered why some people say that becoming a Christian made them feel worse about life? This heightening of our sense of insecurity might be part of this phenomenon. Be sure to understand that I am not saying that we are *less* secure, which would be a lie, I am saying we "feel" less secure. I am also not saying that every person experiences this, but it is common, and can occur to a massive extent or to a minimal level.

This is not a dysfunctional thing; it is part of how God works with us in our lives to draw us toward Him. If you have experienced this, don't slip into a funk because of it. Embrace it and recognize that God is with you and trying to help you overcome the insecurity. The alternative is to slip into negative feelings like worthlessness or inadequacy, which may result in returning to an old addiction or developing a new one. As I've said before, Christians can get trapped.

Now let us move on to Performance the "P" in SPAR. We begin by asking the question, "How do I feel about myself, due to what I do?" This can be a real problem for some Christians. If a person is prone to "performing", Christianity provides immense opportunity to "do things for God", and this can be a danger. In fact, one of the unique Christian doctrines revolves around this very issue, the doctrine of salvation by grace alone.

Just to be sure I'm clear on this let me state this in summary form. A Christian is "saved" from the punishment for their sins by the death of Jesus, which was the payment He made for all the sins of those who believe in Him. All we have to do is accept that, it is God's gift of grace for all who believe in Jesus. There is nothing we can do, no "works" (a Bible term for activities) we can perform, to earn our way into God's presence.

This is one of those simple and profound things about the Christian life. No person can perform his or her way into God's kingdom. No person can perform his or her way into God's approval. No person can perform his or her way into God's grace. No person can perform his or her way into God's acceptance. No person can perform his or her way into God's love. So why do we sometimes try to do it?

Yes, why do we do it? At the root of this is a "Heart" problem, one that involves our belief system. Christianity says that we are saved by our belief in Christ's finished work on the cross. Beliefs are a characteristic of the Heart, as we discussed in the early chapters of the first book. Some people who perform for God do so because their belief system doesn't fully accept the "no performance necessary" guarantee from God about being saved.

I think the level of disbelief ranges from mild to severe. Taking the worst case first, which is complete disbelief, it is easy to see how a person who doesn't believe the doctrine of grace might think that they need to "do things for God" to get accepted, because it is one of the ways we get accepted by our fellow human beings. Then there is the person who may have heard the truth about grace, but has not fully accepted it or just finds it too simplistic. He or she can "perform for God" just in case they haven't understood it properly. Then there is the person who knows what the Scriptures say, but "performs" to show that they are "approved" by God. The reality is that there are many variations of this performance problem, performing for the wrong reason, which we can see in the church. Let's look at some.

I suppose the most obvious one might be performing on stage. This can involve performing as musicians, or as pastors, or as prayer leaders, or as announcement makers. I would also add to the list Christian performers, entertainment artists and TV evangelists, for example, that we see in the Christian world. These are all the people who represent the face of Christianity to us, but also to others outside the church.

Let me be clear here. The people I'm looking at here would be performance driven no matter what they choose to do in life. Performing for acceptance will be covered shortly. The performers in Christianity though, have a serious question to deal with. First they must come to terms with the truth that they are performance driven. Then the question is, "Am I doing this for God, or am I doing this for the satisfaction of my own feelings?" This is a hard question to answer for any person involved in ministry or work done for the advancement of the kingdom of God.

Some answers become clear in time. If a performance driven person is working to resolve his or her feelings, eventually they will not be able to continue their work. They may experience a waning of a passion, or burn out or most likely, no or limited successful results from their work. It is here that the likelihood of "performing for God" can slip someone toward an emotional prison.

As the "working for God" performance driven person continues past the point where they need to stop, they keep going. Now though they have put themselves on a hamster wheel, and have to do more or do it better to become emotionally satisfied. They can easily slip into some form of self-medication to get emotional relief; this can include drinking, drugs or pornography. In fact it would not be a surprise to me to discover that these kinds of struggles can be found in the lives of many church leaders. This then raises extra problems; for example, how would a pastor be able to admit he uses pornography? It would destroy his ministry, his work, the very place he gets most of his feelings resolved. He would then also have to deal with the guilt, resulting in further trouble in his own Soul.

This is where I'm going to stop discussing the "performing for God" problem. One thing I want to suggest is that all Christians stop reading and pray for the individuals in spiritual authority over them. My prayer is that if any of them are struggling with "performing for God" that Jesus will help them resolve it appropriately. Your prayer can be similar to mine, or maybe God would have you pray a different one. We must always remember to pray for our church leaders, and this seems like a good time to do that, and a good specific issue to pray about.

Our next SPAR factor is Acceptance and we ask, "How do I feel about myself due to my perception of what others feel and think about me?" I think this is probably the strongest influence over the behavior of

Christians of the four factors. I have seen it at work at even the youngest of ages. For example, we have all heard testimonies of people who "went forward to accept Christ" or some variation of that at a young age. Then when they get older they have to admit that they made this choice because all of their friends were doing it or something similar. I can't say whether the person at that young age gave their life to Christ or not, but I can say that it was their need for acceptance and approval that pushed them forward. This is why I have heard so many teens and adults get honest by admitting they need to rededicate their lives, or simply accept Christ for the first time. They know that it wasn't the need for God working in them as a child that caused them to seemingly "come to Christ"; it was something else. As they matured, they were able to revisit the original choice without the need for acceptance from other people being a factor.

Earlier in this chapter I discussed how some leaders within the Christian world preach a message that doesn't match what the Bible actually says. I talked about how we see denials of truth, doctrine, grace, faith and application. We now come to what I think is the single most important reason this happens, the search for approval in the deniers. Almost every person who preaches and teaches in these denials will also deny that their need for acceptance from other people is driving them.

Let me go through how it happens. Have you ever noticed how some people say off the wall or controversial statements to get attention? I know that I've done it, and maybe you have too. Well, in that situation a person might get noticed by a few others, which can be the beginning of acceptance from those other people, at least in the mind of the speaker. If the sense of acceptance sticks in the Heart of the individual who spoke the controversial words, they might continue to speak them or make new statements to feed the need.

In the Christian world, putting forward a new interpretation of Scripture, which is most often a form of denial, is just the situation I've described. The speaker might deny that the resurrection took place, which of course is a theological error, and this would certainly get him or her some attention. This could lead him or her to feel accepted. I see this in the work of the "Jesus Seminar" group that I mentioned earlier. Their work is fatally flawed, but they continue to grab attention whenever they can, seeking acceptance. In my opinion the whole "word of faith" movement in Christianity revolves around this issue of acceptance.

The problem with this in Christianity is that these people who operate in error mislead others into what I have called "shooting the wounded" and also into "stinking thinking." All because of a deep seated need for acceptance. The results of this misleading can be disastrous. Some people don't seek medical help for their kids, resulting in death. Others might go to Vegas to get rich and gamble away their money, as they believed the preacher when he said, "God wants you to be rich." Others might go into debt by buying a big house and car when they can't afford it, resulting eventually in bankruptcy. The possible emotional prison aspects of this problem are numerous, and all because some individuals operate their life driven by this desire for acceptance that lingers deep within their Soul.

Our last SPAR factor is Responsibility. The question here is, "How do I feel about myself, due to my ability to meet certain standards?" This is where something called legalism can be a major guilt inducing force. The perceived inability to meet "certain standards" can be used by people who lead groups to develop some level of control over the group. Also some of us internalize "certain standards" and almost whip ourselves because we don't meet them.

First let us see what is going on with the controllers. Since we are talking in the context of Christianity, the controllers are most likely to be "front people" like preachers, teachers and TV talking heads. What they've all discovered, and this can be conscious or sub-conscious, is that some people's inability to "follow the rules" of Christianity causes a response in them of feeling guilty or ashamed. This makes them vulnerable to being led by individuals who promise, and maybe sometimes even deliver, the help to assuage their guilt or shame ridden Hearts. This leads to a level of dependency on the controller, who points to himself or herself as having the answer to the problem. This is what is sometimes known as a false gospel, because the poor wretch with the guilt laden Heart is not pointed at Jesus. Jesus can actually remove the guilt and shame, and not just temporarily reduce any pain that might go along with it, which is all the controller can do.

The outcome for the controller is that he or she is on a path that will take him or her further away from true Christianity as time goes by. As they move away from truth, like the deniers of truth I talked about earlier, they will themselves become vulnerable to feeling the guilt and shame of inadequacy. I know it sounds peculiar, but they almost become a victim of their own messages. They are preaching this "false gospel" and believe it, and yet they will be scouring the real gospel, the Bible, for new ways to package their message. One of the mysteries of the gospel will begin to exert its power in due time as the controller comes face to face with grace. He or she will have to change their ways or begin to medicate their own Soul in some way. This self-medication is the beginning of a journey toward an emotional prison.

The outcome for the controlee or follower is that these vulnerable people do get temporary relief from the negative feelings they have from not being able to measure up. In the end, temporary relief doesn't deal with the real problems that go with negative feelings. But during this period of temporary relief some dysfunctional behaviors can develop that cause trouble. An example of this would be giving so much money to the "cause", whether it is the controller's church or his or her ministry, that the regular bills don't get paid. Another outcome for the follower is that they might be persuaded to spend so much time in supporting the "cause" that they neglect their family. A third and more sinister outcome could be that the controller actually persuades the follower to engage in an illegal or illicit activity. Examples of this include fraud, fleecing the flock, or some form of sexual immorality like an affair with the controller. These behaviors, of course, are symptomatic of emotional prisons!

Some individuals try to deal with the "R" factor by themselves. These are the ones I said "whip" themselves. Not matching up to certain standards is a problem that every human faces, but some of us seem to let it get a grip on us, emotionally speaking. We allow negative feelings about ourselves to arise within our Soul and overwhelm us. I got the word "whip" from thinking about how monks used to flagellate themselves in times past to drive the sins out of their bodies. We still do that today, but it is a little subtler. We read all the Christian self-help books we can, which is ironic since that is what this book is! We pray unendingly, saying the same thing over and over. We listen to all the sermons we can, trying to get something out of the messages that will help. We talk endlessly about our problems to anyone who will listen, sometimes driving away people who care. All of these behaviors are compulsive and can lead us into a deeper place such as a depression.

Some of us discover that if we take a little wine, our feelings disappear for a while, and at least we feel temporarily better. For others it might be prescription pills, or pornography. The whole point here is that an incorrect view of the message Jesus gives us from the Scriptures can lead to an emotional prison. My personal view is that legalism, the unhealthy focus on rules, is an emotional trap in its own right. But it is also true that legalism can lead to other emotional prisons.

Last Points

This is where I try to summarize the chapter. I have attempted to persuade the reader to think about the dysfunctions within the Christian world, and then to see how these dysfunctions work to move us into emotional prisons.

Christianity itself is not dysfunctional, it is the people who practice it, and it is us. We can be lazy, allowing others to tell us what the Bible says without looking for ourselves. We can follow the church and its leaders instead of Jesus, in other words, follow the imperfect instead of the perfect. We can allow negative or erroneous messages in through the gateway of our Soul, resulting in negative feelings.

We Christians have a responsibility toward each other. We have to combat the deniers with truth. We have to not participate in the shooting of the wounded, and we have to expose "stinking thinking." These are things we can do to reduce the possibility of ourselves, our friends and our loved ones falling into the many emotional prisons our world has.

Christianity itself in not an emotional prison, but the malpractice of it can nudge people toward one. As we will find out in the third book, Christianity actually provides the keys to getting out of prison.

This concludes the three-chapter look at religion, in its many facets. My personal view is that religion is the most dangerous of all emotional prisons. It is also the most difficult to get out of since it involves having to radically change the values, beliefs and attitudes found within a Heart.

15

FALSE INTIMACY

Intimacy is being seen and known as the person you truly are.
Amy Bloom

When God created us, as we spoke of in Chapter One of the first book, He created us "in His image" and He gave every person a Soul. Part of what He gave every one of us was the gift of the ability and need to relate at a deep emotional level with Him and with other people. We call this intimacy. This chapter is about the activities we undertake that substitute something for real intimacy. We are going to look at these common surrogate actions and see how destructive they are. They are all emotional traps, and together they form the emotional prison of "false intimacy."

Before we can begin to look at activities that lead us away from true intimacy we must first be sure to define and describe what real intimacy looks like. To me, the place to start is with God. In Chapter One we talked about God as being "God in three persons", namely God the Father, God the Son and God the Holy Spirit. Now we are going to spend a moment on the relational intimacy between the three of them.

What we call the Trinity, God in three persons, is a mystery to us, but not a complete mystery. The Bible gives us some clues about what this Trinity is and how it works. Some of these clues relate to our subject in this chapter of intimacy. It is important to understand and believe that God exists, living in true and absolute intimacy. But what does "true and absolute intimacy mean?"

The word "intimacy" in the English language finds it root in the Latin word "intimus" meaning innermost, and "intimus" is the superlative of "interus" meaning inward. The grammar lesson here is important because we can get a correct view of what our word "intimacy" means. "Intimacy" is a noun, a thing, which is derived from "intimate", which is a transitive verb. So "intimacy is the state derived from being "intimate."

Intimacy is the emotional state achieved through the action of being intimate. Being intimate with another person is the continuous and never-ending action of truly revealing one's innermost being to them. Feelings of intimacy occur when (obviously) one person is being intimate with another. These "feelings of intimacy" include closeness, euphoria, peace, joy, security, restfulness, pleasure, connectedness, support and fulfillment. If we sit and reflect on how good all these emotions feel when we have them inside of us, is it any surprise that we will strive to get them back over and over again? Intimacy can only be achieved in relationship; it requires two people, with both persons having intimacy with each other at the same time.

I once heard a speaker say this. "Intimacy can be spoken of like this, into me you see." When you speak that out loud it provides a very practical way of looking at this subject. It is only when two people reveal their innermost beings, by becoming transparent and allowing each other to "see" their innermost thoughts and feelings, that a relatively deep level of intimacy can be achieved.

This is a good point to say something about how we choose to misuse the word "intimacy" in our culture. I hear it used so often in a way that describes a physical action. For example, we say, "he was intimate with her", meaning he had sex with her. The act of sex does not equal intimacy. Sex could be an action that results from feelings that are present with intimacy, but it doesn't have to be. This will be important later. Let me say one more thing here to clarify things.

Intimacy is a matter of the Soul, not of the body.

Now let's go back to our discussion of intimacy and God. I had asked the question, "What is true and absolute intimacy?" God demonstrates it, and it is the complete knowledge of the innermost parts by one person of the Trinity of the other two persons. There is nothing that each of them doesn't know about the others. How can I say this? I can only look at what the Scriptures say, and particularly what Jesus spoke. I have a couple of favorite scriptures that I think speaks to this subject, one minor, and one major, both from the Gospel of John.

Jn 10:30 - I and the Father are one."

This is a simple and informative summary of the intimacy within the Godhead! The Jewish leaders who were listening to Jesus speak immediately knew that He was saying that He was God and they wanted to kill Him for blasphemy. I don't know how clearer Jesus could be about this, He is God and He and the Father "know" one another so intimately that they are to be regarded as one entity. You might have experienced a relationship where you have bonded with someone so well that you thought you knew each other's thoughts. Here, Jesus is talking about that with His Father, except that His relationship was so strong and permanent that nothing could change it.

The major Scripture example I want to look at is found in the prayer that Jesus prayed for the disciples, including those who came later, meaning all who believed in Him after His death. He prayed this right before He was executed. It occupies the whole of Chapter 17 of the Gospel of John, but we will just look at verses 20 through 23:

Jn 17:20-23 - "I do not ask on behalf of these alone, but for those also who believe in Me through their word; that they may all be one; even as You, Father, are in Me and I in You, that they also may be in Us, so that the world may believe that You sent Me. The glory which You have given Me I have given to them, that they may be one, just as We are one; I in them and You in Me, that they may be perfected in unity, so that the world may know that You sent Me, and loved them, even as You have loved Me."

While there is so much to look at from a theological perspective, all I want to say is that intimacy is the whole theme of this passage. Jesus says that He and His Father are one, meaning having total intimacy. He also prays for the disciples to have intimacy with one another and with Him. I included verse 23 here because it identifies the source of the sustaining power of true intimacy, and that is God's love.

There is one thing that needs to be said here which must be grasped and understood. Intimacy within the Godhead is always spoken of by Jesus as between two of the persons. There are three intimate relationships in the Trinity, Father/Son, Son/Spirit and Father/Spirit. It is the same within the human experience, intimacy can only occur between two persons in an open and honest relationship with one another.

My final word on true intimacy, relates to, and is a logical extension of what I just said about God's sustaining power. True intimacy in any relationship requires the ongoing involvement of God. For some that may be a bold statement, for me it is a simple thing to understand.

Strong intimacy can be developed between two people, but it requires the sacrificial love of God to maintain and sustain it.

False Intimacy

A friend of mine, who I will call Jimmy, has a problem with false intimacy that he is actively working on. Jimmy is in his early forties, but this problem started when he was a young teenager. Jimmy was introduced to pornographic magazines by his father. He was not given the magazines; he found them under his parent's bed by accident. The way Jimmy tells his story suggests that both his father and mother looked at them for their own reasons, and there was a good and constantly replenished supply. Jimmy became popular with his schoolmates, as he would bring the magazines to his middle school and then high school. In the early teen years he would take what he considered the best pictures into the bathroom and masturbate. That felt good, he told me, but he remembers feeling like he wanted more.

As Jimmy moved into his mid teens he finally discussed this with a youth pastor at his church. Jimmy and the young pastor had a sexual experience together after they had bonded around this subject. For Jimmy this was unwanted, although he admits it was consensual because he participated. Jimmy stopped going to his youth group and avoided the youth pastor after that. Then teen boy-girl relationships came and went with as much sex in as many ways as possible. All through this time Jimmy was looking at his father's pornography collection.

He then proceeded to move on to college where the sexual activity increased and developed into more of a casual sexual lifestyle, meaning that even shallow relationships weren't always involved. At college Jimmy was able to get his hands on more explicit pornography and still engaged in masturbation, and this is when he also discovered XXX video stores. He would rent the video pornography and watch it by himself, "always alone" is the way he puts it. He would continue to do everything he could to experience sexual fulfillment, and was tormented by a sense of shame when he "acted out." He was addicted to sex.

Jimmy's addiction stopped, or so he thought, when he met his wife. He was so taken with her that he gave up most of his secret life. They started to go to church together, which he only did to please her, and started to have sex together, which she only did to please him. They got married and Jimmy managed to stay away from his old activities - for a while. Then his addiction reared its ugly head again.

Just as it was when Jimmy was a teenager, it was the magazines that started it. One day, feeling alone and down, Jimmy went and bought a magazine from a convenience store on the way home from work, and masturbated. He says that he felt so much better that he did it again the next day. His addiction had grabbed him again! From there it was only a matter of time before he had an affair, then another and another. Soon this wasn't enough, and he started to visit prostitutes when on business trips. Then he started to visit them during the workday. Jimmy was completely trapped!

By accident Jimmy's wife saw some unusual entries on their credit card bills. Jimmy had mistakenly used one in error while entertaining himself at a "gentlemen's club." After confronting him, his wife further discovered that he had some other personal credit cards where the bills got sent to his office, and that he had a separate checking account to pay for his pleasures. Some of his addictive behaviors were paid for by his firm as entertainment expenses. His life was a sorry mess.

Jimmy and his wife, who has her own complementary issues, are now in the recovery phase of their marriage. He is working on his sexual addiction and she is working on her stuff. She chose to stay after seeking wise counsel, although most people would say she had sufficient reason to divorce Jimmy. They are now able to actually work on developing intimacy in their marriage. I am very happy to report that Jimmy and his wife are progressing slowly and purposefully, both as individuals and as a couple. They are working through all the past hurts and current pain together under the guidance of some godly people. I can see real intimacy beginning to be built in their lives.

Why did I tell you this long story? It is because it is full of false intimacy, and because it ends in the hope of a better future. From the moment Jimmy picked up that first magazine he was looking for relational fulfillment as a one-way street, with him taking and everybody else giving. Let us go back to that day when Jimmy first found the pornography and look at how his Soul responded.

Jimmy opened the pages of the magazine and also opened the gateway of his Soul. He allowed in the pictures and began relating to what he saw, resulting in feelings of pleasure, which further resulted in actions giving him further physical and emotional enjoyment. As this process repeated itself, a new set of beliefs were created in Jimmy's Heart. While I can't say exactly what they were, Jimmy himself told me that he believed he was "sort of loved" by those women, and that it was that way throughout the 25 years that all this was going on.

Jimmy felt connected to a series of things and people as he searched for intimacy within his life, and they all gave him temporary pleasure. These temporary pleasures then became barriers for him to real intimacy by substituting themselves for the real thing. Here is a working list of false intimacies, or stated in the context of the book, emotional traps.

- Pornography
- Fantasy
- Physical Self-gratification
- Many sexual and/or emotional relationships
- Homosexual encounters
- Gentlemen's Clubs and Prostitutes

Now let us look at these one by one and see how they can both be temporarily fulfilling but actually destructive to real relationship and intimacy.

Pornography

"It's harmless, it's just a little porn." I have actually heard those words come out of a father's mouth when confronted with the fact that his magazines and video collection were being used by his thirteen year old to entertain school friends. Although this father was defending his own actions in owning the stuff, his statement exemplifies what the culture thinks about this subject, that it is harmless. Well, let us take a look at what happens inside the Soul of people who use pornography.

What is pornography? Webster's dictionary defines it as, "Material, such as books or pictures, that depicts erotic behavior and is intended to cause sexual excitement." Most of us limit our thinking when we consider pornography as simply photographs and videos. It includes written words, as in letters to the editor of popular magazines, or some of the articles in teen magazines about sexual matters and romance novels. It includes popular TV shows that have all their characters dress in ways intended to attract the attention of the opposite sex. It is also found in movies, even when the sex scenes are unnecessary for the storyline. Pornography can be thought of as eye candy.

When we look at pornography, the gateway of our Soul is opened to the visual or verbal message sent by the pornography manufacturer. When I say, "look at" I mean that choice we make to not just notice something and move on, but to linger and enjoy. When we make that choice, which is an action of our Will, it releases stimulating thoughts in our Soul as we connect beliefs from our Heart and knowledge from our Mind. These stimulating thoughts lead to pleasant feelings; we experience emotions such as pleasure, happiness, euphoria, excitement and intoxication. More importantly, some of us experience connection, we feel linked to the object of the pornography such as the person in the picture. If we are carrying emotional pain around from earlier in our life we might also find that the "good" feelings aroused through pornography causes the pain to lessen or disappear, at least for a while. Inside our Soul we falsely believe that we are experiencing intimacy, because these are also some of the emotions associated with it. This is where we start to get hooked.

As we experience the rush we get from looking at this material, we live in the moment with the pleasant feelings. Any old emotional pain we are carrying has been temporarily masked as we have moments of relief from it through the "good" feelings. Then as the pleasant feelings subside we go back to a less excited state and things return to normal, including the pain, but we remember how "good" those feelings were. Then when we have a need to feel connected again, or to get pain relief, we recognize that the pornography we looked at before helped us, so we return to it. We might even just want to experience pleasurable feelings again so we pick up a magazine or watch a movie or get on the Internet to stimulate ourselves. As this process develops we slowly move from the place in our Soul where we occasionally choose to pick up and put down the stimulating material, to a place where we have to do that frequently in order to feel "good" or to relieve the pain. The compulsion has begun at this point and we are on the road to becoming trapped.

As we start to view and relate to this material we might begin to "act out" in other ways involving physical acts of a sexual nature. This is what Jimmy did when he started to masturbate. These actions then add to the emotional benefit that we have started to believe pornography brings us. We have added physical pleasure to the emotional pleasure, which in turn brings more emotional pleasure. The trap has begun to get tighter.

As our use of pornography becomes more compulsive, we start to need to look at it more frequently and we move from mild visualizations to deeper levels to achieve those feelings we were getting when we started. The pictures get more explicit, the videos get racier, and the romance novels get steamier. Our acting out becomes more frequent; we might move from physical self-stimulation to using other people for sexual satisfaction.

As the move to using other people occurs we might also try to copy the actions we have seen in pictures or read in words. We may also look for individuals to act out with that have similar characteristics to the porn actors or actresses. If we have been indulging in same-sex pornography we may begin to experiment with homosexual or lesbian sex acts. We might even believe that these sexual encounters are times of intimacy, but they are not, they are false intimacy.

The place where we go with this deepening compulsion is to addiction. This is when we finally capitulate and surrender to this habit and let it run our lives. At this point we will do anything to get the rush of stimulation, or the relief from emotional pain, from pornography and all that goes with it. This is when the pornography problem starts to get dangerous, not just for the indulging individual, but also for those around him or her.

As the quest for pleasure or pain relief goes deeper our actions can get to the point where we start to harm others. We might harm our family by spending money that either belongs to them or is meant for other budget purposes. We might lie, cheat and steal to get our pornography fix through our workplace. As we act out with other people in illicit sexual encounters, we will eventually contract an unwanted disease. We may even develop a taste for violence, which could lead to us physically hurting or even injuring others. This violence could possibly move to the place where we would commit rape or murder.

I have shown how the simple act of viewing some pornography is not "harmless", it has long-term implications. Not all people will get into the death spiral I have described. Some will stop indulging completely, others will get caught, like Jimmy, and be forced to choose to face the issue. Others will get caught and choose to carry on anyway. Some of these will live a completely sexualized lifestyle. These are the people that visit prostitutes regularly, or go to clubs to meet others looking for or providing sex encounters. They may also jump into some form of casual sex lifestyle, like promiscuousness or homosexuality.

The people who voluntarily choose or are forced to stop and choose are the fortunate ones; they have a chance to get out of the death spiral. Those who choose to continue to stay spiraling are heading for a life totally consumed by the drive to feel good or pain relief through false intimacy. They will never have those needs satisfied. They are trapped in the emotional prison of false intimacy, put there by their own choice to indulge in pornography.

Fantasy

Part of Jimmy's story includes times when he would seemingly "go into his head." To him this meant mentally picturing people and thinking about doing things with them. As Jimmy tells it, there wasn't always sex involved, but it always involved doing something with another person and sometimes he would end up having sex in his Mind. His fantasies often involved people he knew, and weren't restricted to just women, as he sometimes connected with men. It was speaking of these things with his youth pastor all those years ago that finally resulted in his brief homosexual encounter. Although Jimmy says he didn't really "want" to do anything, he went right ahead and acted out anyway, as he fulfilled his fantasy. After just a few encounters Jimmy stopped as he says, "because it wasn't doing anything for me, and I was starting to feel disgusted with myself."

Jimmy's fantasies didn't end there of course, but it does provide an example of what fantasy, as false intimacy, is all about. Webster's dictionary has an excellent definition of fantasy:

- The power or process of creating especially unrealistic or improbable mental images in response to psychological need.

The deep and powerful psychological need to feel intimacy for many people results in making up situations, events and people to fill that need. We have all done this in some way. It may not be in the context of intimacy or sexual fantasies, but we do it in other ways. Every culture in the world has its stories that came out people's Minds. Just think of the "knight in shining armor saving the fair maiden from the dragon" type of stories we have heard since childhood. Every culture has these kinds of stories. Boys grow up thinking about being the knight and girls want to be the maiden that is rescued, and they both want to live "happily ever after." These are stories of searching for intimacy.

Fantasy is the fuel for much of the entertainment industry. Hollywood action movies feed some of the psychological desires in men. Who doesn't want to be Rambo? The man single-handedly routs entire armies, brings the bad guys to justice and saves the prisoners. While action movies are not necessarily about intimacy, and some of them include romantic aspects, they are still fantasy. Chick flicks are all about intimacy though. They are all about searching for connection through relationship. One of my grandkids has a favorite; it is "Sleepless in Seattle", which has to be a modern classic romantic movie. It is totally a "searching for intimacy movie", a little unrealistic maybe, but still a "feel good" story. And, yes I own it, and I enjoy watching it with my wife every Valentine's day!

Have you ever considered how big the romance novel industry is? This massive publishing industry segment caters to one thing, the fantasies that women want to indulge in. Just a look through a couple of these books would show this to be true. Most of them have some kind of impressive looking guy on the cover, which gets the buyer hooked in. The story then is constructed to fuel the imagination of the reader; sometimes it will include steamy sex scenes. These written scenes are often as explicit as any pornography video, and just as damaging to a person's reality.

There are now whole cable TV channels dedicated to feeding this fantasy world for woman, just as there are pornography channels for men. In my opinion the daytime soap operas are also targeting the female fantasy market, much like pornography videos target male fantasy, and are just as dangerous to marriages. The end results are the same, a distorted view of relationships, and a seeking of intimacy in the wrong places and by illegitimate methods.

The danger of fantasy-fuelled false intimacy is as real as it is for pornography. It will result in dissatisfaction with current relationships, and seeking to get intimacy needs met outside of normal boundaries. Just like with pornography, the romance novel addict may "act out" their fantasies in sexual ways. The chick flick or soap opera also leads our fantasies down roads that end in painful events too. This is because the actual reality of life is so much different from the stories of "true love" that often get pictured. How often does a young girl give herself away to a young man who she imagines will be with her forever, only to find out he is less than she imagined him to be?

Possibly the worst kind of fantasies involve wrapping the false intimacy-seeking approach to romance with pornography. This is where a manufacturer of a movie or a romance novel places relationship in with sexual exploits to get the consumer to suck in the lie that romance plus sex equals a fulfilling and intimate relationship. This is not real life; this is a distortion of reality that will result in the negative emotions of hurt, pain and worthlessness.

The false intimacy created by fantasy is as much of a trap as that created by pornography. The emotional prison of false intimacy is just as dark as any real prison.

Physical Self-Gratification

There are several ways to physically satisfy oneself, such as masturbation, eating, drugs, and sadistic activities. Here we are going to restrict ourselves to only considering sexually oriented self-gratification.

Sexual self-gratification does not just happen. It is always in response to an emotional state, which in turn is a response to some form of stimulus that results in our Soul generating thoughts. There is always something that triggers self-gratification. In Jimmy's case it started with pictures of naked women, then the stimulus was pornographic or sexually explicit video. After that, it was his own "imagination" or fantasies, and finally became a combination of all or any of these things.

Another word that has been used to generally describe the many ways to gratify oneself sexually is "autoeroticism." This word carries with it the idea of a spontaneous and self-loving sexual act, as an automatic action taken when needed. Masturbation is a little different from autoeroticism in that it can be something done in a marriage between the man and wife as an intimate act. Sexual self-gratification done in an autoerotic way involves only one person psychologically. The feelings that arrive before, during and immediately after sexual self-gratification mimic those of an intimate sexual relationship. However, since they are accomplished in the absence of an actual relationship no lasting psychological benefits accrue. This is a sign that autoeroticism gives a person a false sense of intimacy.

In the early years of his sexual addiction, Jimmy had managed to equate the action and result of sexual self-gratification with feeling good about himself and his imaginary relationships. This served his need for relationship and intimacy for a while, but because it provided only a false sense of intimacy it was never going to last. As Jimmy found out, there is no substitute for real intimacy. He eventually graduated from pleasing himself through autoerotic behavior to having to use real people in his quest for intimacy.

That is the way it is. Indulging in frequent physical self-gratification is an attempt by an individual to gain the feelings that go with intimacy. The reality is that it will never actually do that since it takes a person down a false trail. This false trail is one where some feelings that seem like they provide a sense of connection are found, but a person on this false trail is alone. Real intimacy can never be experienced by yourself, it can only be found in relationship with other people.

The great benefit, and I hesitate to use that word, of autoerotic behavior is this: It puts an individual in apparent control of everything surrounding the need for intimacy in their life. It allows a person to turn on the feelings of false intimacy whenever they want. It also allows that person to never experience the negative feelings, such as rejection, that are part of an actual intimate relationship. The problem is, autoerotic behavior will never satisfy the Soul's hunger for intimacy because it is always about oneself. Ultimately, an individual gets trapped into indulging in sexual self-gratification to the point that they must do it compulsively. This compulsion is a trap formed through their need to feel the feelings that go with intimacy. It becomes an emotional prison.

Many sexual and/or emotional relationships

What do I mean by this phrase "many sexual and/or emotional relationships?" We all know what I'm talking about here, as it is very common in our culture. We all recognize it by different names and in various word forms. Some of these include:

- Looking for love in all the wrong places
- He's a womanizer
- She's a slut; he's a hound dog

- String of affairs
- Promiscuity

I'm sure that this list could easily be added to!

I've read quite a lot of articles and done some research on this whole subject of why we do this "looking for love" thing. There seems be a consensus or what we call common knowledge that this "acting out" does not actually help except to give a person relief from negative feelings. This is because we are all looking for intimacy, and looking for love provides something that seems to meet our intimacy needs, but it is a lie, a false intimacy.

This is where I met Jimmy. I had yet another emotional affair, which is a relationship with a person who is not your spouse in an attempt to find intimacy. He and I had this common thread, and we discovered this at a recovery meeting we both attended. Jimmy was searching for intimacy through affairs that involved sexual activity; I was searching for the same thing, but through deeper relational affairs. We were both not only "looking for love in all the wrong places", but in wrong ways too!

Although Jimmy's compulsion was similar to mine in the object of what we were both searching for, it was different in the method. He would develop a relationship and if it didn't go to a sexual level quickly, he would move on. This is because he would perceive the feelings that go with sexual activity with a person who seemingly strongly wanted him, as intimacy. This new person seemed to strongly want him because in the first part of a relationship there wasn't typically any baggage, which is accumulated negative feelings. Since there was limited negativeness, everything felt positive and was interpreted as a strong desire by Jimmy.

My case differs in that I too was looking for intimacy, but for me sexual activity wasn't relevant. What I was seeking was relational attachment, a bonding that only comes through a deeper emotional connection than typically happens in a sexual affair. For me the sharing, the to and fro of relationship, and the resulting bonding was everything. That was where I felt my false intimacy.

From the outside Jimmy's pattern of behavior and mine looked very similar - a string of relationships occurred. From the inside they were very different. We were both looking for intimacy but our methods were

73

completely different. We were both trapped in false intimacies, and both in an emotional prison.

I want to talk here to those affected by a person who has been involved in a string of relationships. You could be the person who has done what either Jimmy or I did. You could be the spouse of the offender. You could be a close friend or family member. Whoever you are in this picture please remember this: the offender will never grow or mature out of it by him or herself. The search for intimacy is a lifelong pursuit. This means that getting help from a third party, a non-involved individual, will be necessary. God Himself may directly intervene, but a good alternative would be to seek professional help through a Christian counselor. That is what I did.

Now I want to say a special word for the spouse of someone who has had a series of relationships. There is nothing you could have done to stop this from happening. The person who does this is driven by a need found in every person, the need for intimacy. They are the person who chose to seek it outside of the boundary of the marriage. Whether they admit it or not, they also know that what they did, or are doing, is wrong. But do not give up hope, because there is help on how to deal with this problem and how to heal the broken marital relationship. This hope is found in the healing work done by God through His many mysterious ways. The whole of the last book discusses this.

Homosexual encounters

The whole subject of same-sex relationships that have a sexual component (which I am going to call homosexuality) is extremely controversial in modern American culture. Everything about homosexuality is analyzed to death, and experts from all parts of hard and soft sciences, theologians and psychologists disagree on almost everything about it. There is a constant war going on to make a determination on the question about whether homosexuality is caused by nature or nurture. Within that war there are battles to determine if homosexuality is genetic in origin or has its start in something physical happening in the womb or early childhood. Others take a view that a domineering parent can cause homosexuality. There seems to be a lot of vested interest and a lot at stake in figuring it out, and I think it is all wasted effort as it misses a central focus. Now, let me explain my perspective of homosexuality.

Jimmy's homosexual encounter, put in the context of his whole story, provides us with a really big clue as to what is happening inside the person engaging in homosexual behavior. All the behaviors that Jimmy got involved in were part of his search for intimacy. They were all false intimacies that gave Jimmy a sense of being connected to others. Jimmy's brief same-sex physical activity originated in his quest for intimacy, and is therefore just another part of his "looking for love in all the wrong places."

When I view Jimmy's story and all the other same-sex situations I've personally witnessed, I can now see the same thing. All the people involved were seeking intimacy, as we all are, but these people were seeking it in a way that they weren't designed to. Our design, both physiologically and psychologically, is for intimacy that includes sexual behavior to be experienced only in a heterosexual relationship. The feelings that come into being as a result of same-sex attraction and homosexual behavior are incorrectly recognized as satisfying the need for intimacy by some people. The emotions involved are very real and as they are experienced in relationship can lead some people to continue to seek them over and over. Just as in a heterosexual situation, this "seeking" behavior can lead to many sexual encounters, which is promiscuity, or a single monogamous relationship, and anything in-between.

Understanding this can lead us to a more rational view of homosexuality and the people who practice it. The view that homosexuality is just one possible behavioral attempt at finding intimacy also points to where answers to dealing with it in our own lives or helping others overcome it can be found. Homosexuality is simply the behavioral result of a dysfunction in the Soul brought about by false beliefs involving how to relate to others. When this behavioral issue is understood this way we can then see that it is no different than using pornography, having affairs or living a fantasy life in the pursuit of intimacy.

Homosexuality is a behavior conducted in response to emotions that a person has when involved in a same-sex relationship. Since these emotions, some of which are pleasure, connectedness, fulfillment, and euphoria as a group, feel good. A person will often go back frequently to the homosexual behavior to regain the "feel good" state. This is where the behavior becomes compulsive and ultimately addictive. For this reason homosexuality results in a person being trapped in an emotional prison.

What is a problem for any person engaging in this behavior is the inevitable negative feelings that come along. Because this particular behavior is so obviously not what each of the sexes were designed to do, a myriad of problematical emotions arise. Persons who engage in homosexuality can expect to feel heavy shame and guilt, and also experience a considerable sense of low self-esteem. In short, they are going to be miserable. There are two major ways that most of us deal with miserable feelings; we get depressed or we deny they exist. Sometimes the denial is so strong that we get angry with anyone who points out that our behavior is hurting us. That is, of course, a very strong characteristic of the homosexual community. This makes dealing with this group of people very difficult and the healing of the homosexual person problematical. There is a book reference in the bibliography which helps us to understand these issues more clearly.

I think it is also important to look at the subject of Christians and homosexuality. I cringe when I see what some professed Christians do and say around this subject. I see name-calling and various references to "burning in Hell." I have to admit I get very judgmental of my fellow believers who do this. It seems that for them, homosexuality is a top tier sin, when in reality it is no different to stealing a pen from the office, or telling a lie to your spouse. Let me prove that this is so from the Bible.

Some extremist Christians are fond of quoting this verse:

Lev 18:22 - You shall not lie with a male as one lies with a female; it is an abomination.

This is an obvious reference to male homosexuality, which is called an "abomination", a very bad thing. But these same extremists ignore what it says in the book of Proverbs:

Pr 6:16-19 - There are six things which the Lord hates, yes, seven which are an abomination to Him: Haughty eyes, a lying tongue, and hands that shed innocent blood, a Heart that devises wicked plans, feet that run rapidly to evil, a false witness who utters lies, and one who spreads strife among brothers.

The reality is that all sin is an abomination to God, the size or type does not matter. It is all unacceptable. Homosexuality is a sin, yes, but is must not be singled out as different or worse than any other. What is

76

very important to acknowledge is that homosexuality is a misbehavior resulting from the pursuit of a legitimate goal, intimacy, and that makes it a false intimacy. A second important thing to remember and acknowledge is that because homosexuality is a sin revolving around the strong need for intimacy, it is powerful once it gets a grip on the Soul of an individual. This powerfulness makes escaping the grip of homosexuality very difficult for the person trapped in it. It is truly one of the deepest emotional prisons there is.

Gentlemen's Clubs and Prostitutes

It is the same story here. Individuals who pursue these activities are looking for intimacy. The big difference is that money changes hands as part of the activity.

I personally don't see much difference between the viewing of pornography, which is looking at material goods, and going to a strip joint or a so-called gentlemen's club which is viewing live goods. Either way the person is trying to get their need for intimacy met. Just as in the case of pornography, the visitor to clubs like this will never get satisfied long-term, will probably get hooked, and eventually spend his or her money until they run out.

Jimmy went to prostitutes because he ran out of females who would have an affair with him, and he says he found them very convenient. He would pay a little more for extra time and get more than just sex from them. Once in a while he would quit using them, which was when he found a new partner for an affair. His basic position was that a prostitute was a short-term affair.

If we cast our thoughts back in time and recall all the scandals involving high profile individuals and prostitutes, we can see a pattern. They all spent a considerable amount of time away from their significant relationships, from their normal intimate partners. They were vulnerable and needed intimacy and they chose the lazy way of dealing with it. They chose a substitute intimacy.

Paying for false intimacy has been around a long time. The problem is that after you pay with the credit card, you pay in the Soul. A person who has to use clubs and prostitutes is as trapped as a person who can't give up drugs. They are in an emotional prison, the prison of false intimacy.

A Word On Intimacy Needs

For those that want to delve into intimacy more thoroughly, there are some books available that center around the concept of intimacy needs. These resources, which I have listed in the bibliography, are helpful in understanding what intimacy is, how it develops in us, how to parent with it in mind and how to go about developing it.

The work, based on Christian spiritual principles, shown in these books center on the idea that we all have "intimacy needs", and lists the ten most important. These are; Acceptance, Affection, Appreciation, Approval, Attention, Comfort (meaning empathy), Encouragement, Respect, Security and Support. I have also listed the web address for the ministry that has grown around the idea of developing biblically based intimacy in the home. This may be particularly helpful for those struggling with intimacy in marriage.

SPAR and False Intimacy

It is the four SPAR factors that are primarily responsible for us falling into an emotional prison. There is typically one dominant factor, but some of us may have more than one operating in our lives. In the case of false intimacies, there is truly one dominant factor, and that is "Acceptance", with a minor factor of "Security." So let's look at these false intimacies from these two perspectives.

I'll start with the minor factor of "Security." One of the characteristics of an intimate relationship is that the people in it have a healthy sense of personal security. It may be better thought of as a result of an intimate relationship when trust and empathy build between two people. When a person has a good Soul-to-Soul connection with another, he or she can rely on the other to be there when things are tough. The Mind of each of them develops knowledge and understanding about the benefits of this relationship. The Heart of each also develops beliefs, values and attitudes about the healthy and close connection it has with this other person. These things together add up to an internal sense of comfort, supportiveness and trust which manifests itself as feeling secure.

When a person does not carry around a healthy sense of personal security, he or she is vulnerable to false intimacy. In Chapter Nine of Emotional Prisons – Origins we discussed how the teen years are a time of significant personal insecurity. That insecurity is why the adolescent is particularly susceptible to things like pornography and unhealthy sexual relationships, or in fact any false intimacy. Our society instinctively knows and understands this, which is why we have laws to protect our teenagers from some of these false intimacies. We try to guard their Souls from the very damaging effects of some of the problems I talked about earlier.

Let's consider some of the things that parts of our society do to try to invade the Minds and Hearts of our teens for their own selfish purposes. The pornography industry is constantly seeking to break down society's boundaries in providing material to teens younger than eighteen. This is because it knows that if it can capture their Soul into the trap of this false intimacy, it will gain a consumer for life, or at least for a long time. The homosexual community is always probing for ways to introduce the concept of same-sex sexual relationships as "normal" to teenagers. This is part of a longer-term plan to try to get our culture to accept homosexuality as a normal and healthy lifestyle.

The big, and I mean big, problem with both of these is that the end result will be the degrading of our society. What happens is that these false intimacies literally will destroy the ability of a person to function productively as they succumb to the compulsions and addictions that develop. Instead of producing healthy families or going to work and earning a living, some of the trapped individuals will choose to engage their compulsions. How much of this can our culture take before we eventually break down, being eaten from the inside out?

I am not being alarmist here. I volunteer in a recovery ministry, and I hear the stories from men like Jimmy every week. I hear stories of addictions to pornography, same-sex attractions and use of prostitutes. In all of these stories I hear the results. Results like the spending of the family's money to engage in the compulsions, like fantasizing about sexual relationships with other people and like using the office computer to view pornography. Each of these things takes something away from others as they serve to feed an individual's false intimacy needs. False intimacy has the power to destroy the American culture.

The biggest internal driver in the pursuit of false intimacies is acceptance. In his book "The Search for Significance", Dr, Robert McGee uses the term "Approval Addict" to describe this. We are so driven by our need to be approved and accepted by others that we will do almost anything to get it. Acceptance is a big part of intimacy, acceptance of who we are, not what we do. If a sense of acceptance is not present in our Souls, we will attempt to find it somewhere and that place is often in a false intimacy.

I've lost count of the number of times I've heard a man say something like, "when I was looking at pornography I felt connected and accepted by the person in the picture." Some people who read that would say that that statement is ridiculous or preposterous. Please don't do that - false intimacy is a powerful thing. When a person is desperate for acceptance, it means they feel they need it from somewhere just to get through the day. When they get that needy, they will take acceptance even from a picture. To understand this we have to see what the needy person sees. They see a pretty girl or guy in a sexually alluring pose, an inviting position that is experienced as "I want you" in the Soul of the viewer. This is an excellent example of allowing something dangerous through the gateway of the Will into the Soul where it starts to form new false beliefs in the Heart.

Starting with that moment of acceptance, experienced as intimacy, the needy person has then begun the slip down the slope of relying on false intimacies to meet their emotional need for acceptance. It becomes a short emotional trip to the point of self-gratification, and then it has begun; the spiral downward into compulsive use of false intimacy to "feel better." The person who gets some sense of intimacy from these initial encounters with pictures and self-gratification has a place to go, emotionally speaking, whenever they want to feel better. The problem, as we have said before, is that because this is a false intimacy, ultimately it will not satisfy, and will actually end up doing the opposite; it will leave a person empty.

As we have seen previously the need for acceptance from others is a powerful emotional force in our lives. Nowhere is it more dangerous to us than when we try to meet it though false intimacy. False intimacies will trap us and produce bad fruit in our lives. It will destroy relationships, be the root cause of financial bankruptcy, get us thrown into jail and cause us to contract life changing diseases like AIDS. False intimacies are truly treacherous and are emotional prisons.

A Warning From Scripture

The Scriptures warn us about this issue of false intimacies. The oldest book of the Bible, the book of Job, says it well:

Job 31:1-3 - I made a covenant with my eyes, not to look lustfully at a girl. For what is man's lot from God above, his heritage from the Almighty on high? Is it not ruin for the wicked, disaster for those who do wrong? NIV

What a simple and straightforward way to tell us where false intimacy will lead us. It starts with lust, a condition of the Soul, where we are thinking and feeling about getting our needs met in a self-centered way. And it ends in ruin or disaster for those who do it.

The next time you are tempted to take the world's view that a little porn is okay, or prostitution should be legalized, or that gentlemen's clubs are just for fun, or that homosexuality is just another lifestyle, remember this. It all ends in ruin and disaster. I'm going to say it again, false intimacies are treacherous and they are emotional prisons.

16

ADDITIVES

In the 1960s, people took acid to make the world weird. Now the world
is weird, and people take Prozac to make it normal.
Author Unknown

As we have explored the world of emotional prisons we have seen that
all of us respond to the internally generated emotions that rise up in our
Soul. Mostly we respond in a thoughtful, socially acceptable and
harmless way. Some of us don't do so well and we "act out" as in "act
out of our emotions." "Act out" is a term we generally use to describe
the actions we take in response to our own emotions that is harmful to us
or others. With "additives", the subject of this chapter, there is an
additional component.

I used to work in a refinery, and one of the things that we did was to add
chemicals to the refined products. There were three major reasons we
did that. The first reason was to fix the product so that it wouldn't
deteriorate in quality. The second was to deal with instability of the
products, for example to reduce the risk of fire. The third was to boost
performance, to make things run smoother, faster, hotter or more
efficiently. We called these chemicals - yes you guessed it, "additives."

In the context of this book I am going to use "additives" to describe
anything chemical we use to accomplish one of these three emotional
objectives:

1. Sustain our emotional condition
2. Stabilize our emotional state
3. Boost emotional performance

We will talk more about these three below, but first, a good question to
answer at this point is, "What exactly are the additives you are talking
about?" Most of us instantly could come up with a typical list like this:

- **Alcoholic drinks, such as beer, wine and liquor**

- **Legal drugs, such as painkillers, antidepressants and amphetamines**
- **Illegal drugs, such as cocaine, heroin and speed**
- **Inhaled airbornes, such as tobacco (nicotine) and marijuana (THC)**

That would probably be the end of it for most discussions about drugs and alcohol, but we need to dig deeper. When we do, we can come up with more things to add to the list:

- **Anabolic Steroids, typically used by athletes**
- **Household chemicals, such as paint thinner**
- **Man made vitamins, such as "B1 and B2" for stress**
- **Herbal concoctions, such as Valerian for anxiety**

When we really sit and ponder this issue, there is one major class of emotion altering additives that is not given the attention, in the context of impacting emotions, that it ought to have, it is:

- **Food and Drink.**

That is right; I have just added a coke and ice cream to the same list as cocaine and alcohol!

Before we take a detailed look at the three emotional objectives, it is prudent to consider two things: The body to Soul connection, what is it, how does it work and how does it relate to emotions. Then we'll look at the question of what additives do to us to affect our emotional condition.

The Body to Soul Connection

I must admit this is a difficult subject to get my head around, because I don't understand it to a level that satisfies me. I actually regard this body to Soul connection as somewhat of a mystery. Still, I'm going to speak to it as far as I can because it is important to know certain things about it.

The place to start is asking ourselves the question, what is it? This is my answer. It is an affective relationship between the body and Soul. This means that one has the ability to affect the other. When I was sitting and pondering over this whole subject, I became aware of just what an amazing statement that is. It is amazing because it proves how well designed we are. Let me share some relevant things about this.

Our body is a biochemical masterpiece, but by itself it can only function as designed; that is as a rational biological entity. It will process food to sustain itself, it will reproduce itself through sexual activity, and then it will die through natural deterioration. We have this in common with animals; we are all hard wired to do these things. The difference between animals and us is that we have a Soul.

The Soul, somehow contained within the body, is able to alter the normal functions of the body. Let me give you some examples. A person can choose if he or she wants to eat or fast, an animal will not do this. When attacked an animal is likely to fight or flee, but humans can choose to do neither. When it is time to mate, an animal will engage in sexual activity - a human can choose to do that or not. I'm sure every person that reads this could come up with more examples.

It is the Soul that separates us from other created beings. Humans have all the nine attributes of the Soul available to help direct the body; animals do not. As a reminder these attributes are knowledge, understanding, wisdom, values, attitudes, beliefs, control, choice and gateway. We humans apply these to our lives by how we direct our body to function.

There are times when the body can, at least temporarily decide what to do for itself. We normally call this instinct. A good example is when we see a snake on the path in front of us we would normally have an immediate physical reaction as the biochemical response kicks in. Another is when we see a ball coming toward our head, we duck. In my examples we don't wait to evaluate how we are feeling or what we are thinking, we just do it.

When I weigh all these things I see that our Soul is in charge of our body. It directs our bodily activities; it makes the choices about what the body is to do. However, the body has some built-in processes that are designed into it, and some of these can influence and, in certain circumstances, overrule what the Soul might normally choose. This is where additives come in.

There is a very interesting verse of Scripture that comes to mind here:

3 Jn 2 - Beloved, I pray that in all respects you may prosper and be in good health, just as your Soul prospers.

I'm not a Bible scholar, so take this with the understanding that what I am about to say is my personal view of what the Bible is saying here.

It seems to be that the Apostle John writes here that there is some link between the health of the Soul and the health of the body, and also prosperity (which may or may not be material in nature). I personally think there is because of my life experiences. I have seen many cases of people who are troubled by their emotions who take additives and suffer as life goes along, particularly in their health. I'm sure we all know smokers and drinkers who have health problems. The root cause is not the additive, it is the unresolved emotions. I have also met many others who do try to deal with their emotions and seem to get through life well, and without additives to help! It is an interesting question.

What Additives do!

Assume that we all understand we need certain levels of thousands of additives to maintain the home of our Soul. These are important for our body to function as our creator intended. I am going to label these as necessary additives, and I want to speak to them for a moment or two.

Necessary additives include all the chemicals you might expect. Carbohydrates, vitamins, trace minerals and water. There are literally thousands of these chemicals. What is true of all of them is that if a person gets too much of them it will negatively affect their physical health, even to the point of death. It is also true that too little may also cause a person's physical health to deteriorate, also sometimes to the point of death.

I think we can all agree that when a person has too much or too little of some of these necessary additives their emotional state can be affected. This simply states the obvious - what we do to our bodies can affect our Soul. Do you remember a time you were sick as a kid because you had too much chocolate? Yes, chocolate does contain many necessary additives, but that is not the point of the question. The point is; your body was affected to the point that your Soul was influenced so that you probably vowed to never do that again.

In my "chocolate" example, the body's biological and biochemical processes were overwhelmed by all those extra and unnecessary chemical additives it was getting. The body is programmed or designed to react to this through various mechanisms like causing a person to throw up or to cease eating or maybe to sleep. The Soul, which resides in the body, will also respond by opening up its gateway to the information that the body, its home, is under stress because of an action that has occurred. The Soul will then process the information and come up with thoughts and emotions. Each Soul will internally respond in its own way, as determined by the unique combination of beliefs, attitudes, values, knowledge and understanding that it has. It might say, internally responding to what happened, something like "I'll never do that again" or "That felt bad, but it was worth it."

In my fun example of eating chocolate we can see a simple truth that the state of our Soul is changed as a response to the overeating of the chocolate. The thinking state and emotional condition of the Soul is changed as a response to the body's reaction to chocolate. This is the key to understanding additives.

Additives change the thinking and emotional condition of the Soul!

I want to look at three aspects of this statement:

- Quality, of what we add to our body
- Quantity, how much we add
- Frequency, how often we add these to our system

When we think about quality we typically are considering one of two things, the character of an item or the excellence of an item. A relevant example is a vitamin. Which is a better quality, a vitamin made in a lab or the same vitamin found in a fruit? Would you prefer Vitamin C from an orange or Vitamin C made in a chemical plant?

Now how about this aspect of quality, if you drink alcohol would you prefer beer, wine or liquor as your additive? The character of these three types of alcoholic drinks are all different, they have different qualities. How about illegal drugs? Isn't cocaine different to heroin? What about legal drugs, don't Percodan and Vicoden do the same things to us but have different qualities?

Moving on to quantity, generally speaking the more we take in of something the more we will be affected, but this is not always true. We only need a small amount of Vitamin C and adding more won't affect us very much as the body can cope with the excess. If we gave ourselves enormous amounts we would most likely get really sick.

With alcohol or drugs though, it is true that the more we have the more we will be affected. In fact when we drink or drug, we are usually trying to be affected, we are trying to change our emotional state. How many of us have said in our Minds, or even out loud, something like this, "I think I'll have an extra drink, I'll feel better." The problems come of course when we overdo the quantity, our thinking and feelings are so affected we cannot function well. When we really overdo it, our body may shut down or even lapse into a death.

Lastly I want to look at frequency. We all know that we are supposed to add Vitamin C to our bodies on a daily basis, to achieve the best physical results. We also know that in the short term this won't really affect us in the sense of our emotional state. In the long term though a lack of Vitamin C will first damage our health and would then probably affect how we feel emotionally. For example we might develop scurvy, the disease that comes as a result of a lack of Vitamin C. This results in skin spots and spontaneous bleeding, and when it gets worse you lose your teeth, and have non-stop diarrhea. I think you might agree that these things will affect your emotional state.

What about legally prescribed drugs? In most cases the frequency of dosage has been carefully tested to achieve optimal results. If we veer off course and alter the frequency of dosage, things can happen that we had not planned. If you take cholesterol lowering drugs you might begin to have liver failure when you take too much, or high cholesterol when you take too little. Ultimately your physical health, very likely followed by your emotional health, deteriorates. The same would be true of most prescribed drugs. This deterioration is most profound in drugs actually designed to alter your emotional state. Drugs like psychotropics such as Lorezopam for anxiety work really well, but if you mess with the frequency of dosage things like aggressive behavior, physical agitation or even suicide can occur. These are obvious actions based on the emotional state of the Soul, the person on the drug "acts out" under its influence.

The same kinds of problems occur with most illegal drugs or even herbal products. Small amounts of them we can cope with physiologically and psychologically, but high frequency of dosing may cause horrible side effects. For example, cocaine use can lead to significant heart problems, even to the point of a heart attack, and it also leads to paranoid psychosis, such as feelings that people are out to get you.

Now I am going to get to the point, which is probably quite obvious. Starting with my earlier statement that "Additives change the thinking and emotional condition of the Soul", we can now add to it to make it a little more informative.

Additives change the thinking and emotional condition of the Soul. The extent of the change is mostly determined by the quantity, quality and frequency of additive use.

It is time to finalize our answer to the question of what additives do. It is this; in the early part of the book we have seen that each Soul is unique. Every Soul is unique because it was created that way, and it is unique because it has its own life experiences. As a result each Soul will respond to any situation in a unique way.

In the context of additives, one person, a Soul, might respond to an offer of drugs with a "no" and another might say, "Okay, I'll try it." Then after taking the drugs, one Soul might respond with an emotional sense of feeling out of control, whereas another might feel euphoric. The responses of our Soul largely determine if we will allow ourselves to return to the additives we have tried. All the "Just say no" programs we put our kids through are based on this "Soul response" truth. We want to protect them from experiencing the effects of drugs by training their Soul to say "no" as its response to the offer of drugs. Whether the programs work or not is hard to gauge, but we must continue to send these messages into the gateway of the Soul of our children if we want to be responsible as parents.

In summary, "What Additives Do" is this:

Additives change the thinking and emotional condition of the Soul. The extent of the change is mostly determined by the quantity, quality and frequency of additive use. The actual change of the thinking and emotional state of the Soul is established as a distinctive response through the unique nature of an individual's Soul.

In the context of the subject of this book we can now see the obvious, things we put in our body can change our emotional state. Let's explore this by looking at the three emotional objectives a person might have for his or her use of additives.

Three Emotional Objectives

In the introductory part of this chapter I established three emotional objectives that a person might have for his or her use of additives. These are:

1. **Sustain our emotional condition**
2. **Stabilize our emotional state**
3. **Boost emotional performance**

Before we go on I want to be sure to recognize that in any given situation it is possible that a person may be seeking to achieve just one or a combination of these three objectives. Also for clarification I am going to use the word "objective" in a qualitative way, meaning that it has no defined quantitative or specific aspect. As an example, a person might have an objective of going to the Himalayas to climb mountains, but a specific goal of climbing Mount Everest.

Sustaining Our Emotional Condition

The first emotional objective is, "Sustain our emotional condition." There are moments in life when we just want to stay exactly where we are, in an emotional sense. Can you remember some of them? How about that first time you really connected with a person you thought you loved, and you wanted it to last forever, or, maybe when your team had just won the championship. Have you ever been on a mountaintop and looked down on everything as you felt on top of the world. Maybe you have experienced the powerful feeling of being in a major thunderstorm with all the lightning around you. On the darker side perhaps you have wanted to stay in the agony of a first broken love relationship. Maybe you have lost a child or a spouse and felt like you don't want to go on. Perhaps you have wanted to stay in the feelings of guilt and shame you have experienced after realizing you have done something very wrong. And in the middle of these extremes, some of us would like to keep experiencing the peaceful and restful emotional conditions we can get from time to time.

These are all examples of emotional conditions we can find ourselves in that we want to hold on to, that we want to sustain, for our own personal reasons. All of us knows that these emotional conditions never last. We are not able, within ourselves, to hold on to those feelings that go with the emotional conditions we are in.

I must admit here though that some people seem to be able to maintain certain emotional conditions. The important word here is "seem." When we examine what is really happening there is more going on than the continuation of a desired emotional state. Consider the person who seems to want to stay depressed and manages to stay there. When you actually inspect what is happening you can see that they have changing emotional states like everyone else, but choose to find circumstances that are likely to bring back the "down" feelings. (I also want to acknowledge here that some people have a seemingly permanently depressed state due to the malfunctioning biochemical action of the body.)

I said a couple of paragraphs ago that we all know we cannot hold on to the feelings that go with these desired emotional states, within ourselves. So some of us turn to "additives" to try to stay where we are, emotionally speaking. We might want to continue to feel euphoric or "high" so we might take a little 4-MAR, which is an unregulated drug known to produce a long lasting state of feeling high. Perhaps we would prefer to maintain the "peaceful easy feeling" that the Eagles sang about in their 1972 hit. We might turn to Kava-Kava, a natural root extract that seems to help us maintain a sense of relaxation. For those who are trying to stay in a "down" state, how about taking Valium or Librium on a long-term basis?

The point here is that there are additives, chemicals you can smoke, inject, eat or swallow, to help try to maintain any given emotional state. The worldwide drug industry, in all its forms, relies on us all wanting to maintain our emotional states. While they would never admit this, what they do is to help us move into an emotional prison. The prison of being trapped in an addiction to certain emotional states, with the additives being the walls and roof that keep us there.

Stabilizing Our Emotional State

Our second emotional reason or objective is, "To stabilize our emotional state." From an emotional perspective most of us experience life as an uneven series of ups and downs. This is, of course, just the way life is. We all have seasons when things seem to go well and we feel mostly encouraged, positive or even excited. There are also seasons when the feelings are more of discouragement, negativeness or depressing. These seasons can last for a few minutes or a few months, but rarely seem to go on beyond that. I like to think of these as big emotional waves, like the waves you see surfers on, which start way out and seem to take a long time to come to shore where they finally fade away.

Some of us don't experience the big waves like that. For some of us the waves are more like the ones that come with tropical storms. Tropical storm waves are generated and maintained by several strong forces; the winds, the temperatures and the tides. These waves come crashing into the shoreline and present a picture of chaos and volatility in nature. That is the way it is for some of us emotionally. We live through life as if it was one continuous series of tropical storms of feelings. Sometimes we surge and feel powerful, other times we come crashing down on the rocks.

The "emotional tropical stormer" may choose to live with the roughness of his or her emotional volatility. They may also learn to cope with it and achieve some sort of control over their tempestuous emotional life. However, some don't choose to rein in their emotions, they choose to use the calming power of certain additives.

Something to understand about the "emotional stormer" is that they look like the rest of us. Oh yes, they certainly can be outwardly volatile, but they are most likely not. I knew a man, we'll call him Jim, who was a closet "stormer", and nobody really knew that. He discovered that when he got into an emotional storm a quart of Haagen Daas ice cream calmed him down. It had to be that brand; nothing else did it for him! Jim would call it his comfort food, but he would also say it calmed him down. It is clear that it wasn't comfort food, it was calming food. Without realizing it this became Jim's way of dealing with life's troubles. He eventually became more compulsive about his ice cream habit to the point that he put on some serious weight. Just so the reader knows, Jim did quit, but he was still a stormer, and he developed other unhealthy ways of coping. This is called "substitution", where we substitute one compulsive behavior for another.

There are many Jims out there. They don't all use ice cream of course; legal and illegal drugs, and even some herbs, that help with emotional storming are plentiful. Our culture has typically referred to these as "uppers" and "downers", and a large number of these have been synthesized over the last forty years.

The most common "upper" classification is amphetamines. People use these uppers when they are in the downside of their emotional wave. An example would be when we are feeling "down" or "blue." Most commonly it seems to be normal to start to use uppers when life has "become a drag", meaning it is boring. An "upper" is a chemical method of lifting a person's spirits or improving their mood, just add some to your body's biological system and hey prèsto you feel better.

Common legal amphetamines include Adderall, Vyvanse and Dexedrine. Illegal products of this type, made in "meth" labs, include speed, ice, crystal and crank. They all work on our bodies by mimicking the effect of the hormone adrenalin. They bring your biological processes up, which is of course why they are called uppers. The problem is, after you've come up, you go back down when they wear off. This is where the real problem begins. Once a person has discovered that he or she can eliminate or reduce the down emotional times with an additive, they want to do it again. This is the beginning of the addiction and it is an emotional prison.

There also appears to be some link between sugar and high activity levels in children. In a study done in the 1990s at Yale University it was noted that high levels of glucose in children resulted in high levels of adrenaline being produced. This apparently was more pronounced when the origin of the glucose was refined sugar, such as is found in candy and soft drinks. High levels of adrenaline are associated with high levels of activity. (By this time every parent is saying, duh!) The point here is that when we allow our children to consume refined sugar we are giving them an "upper." Is it any wonder that our nation's kids like to consume sweet stuff? It results in them feeling better. Unfortunately, it may also put them on a path to an emotional prison as they learn to rely on ingesting something to feel more alive.

On the other side of the storm we have a class of products called "downers." These are designed to bring a person down from the top of the waves found in emotional storms. This could be when a person is anxious, or can't sleep. Or maybe they feel like life is going along too fast, or that they are under too much pressure. In this instance they may turn to something to bring them down, emotionally speaking, by using a "downer." Sometimes a person who has been using "uppers" may rely on "downers" to chemically adjust their mood to what they might consider normal.

There are many variations of "downers", which perhaps is a chemical comment on the nature of modern society. "Downers" can be generally classified into two broad groups; tranquilizers and sedative-hypnotics. Tranquilizers, of course, are designed to tranquilize the person who takes them. This is simply an attempt to use chemicals or additives to calm down. Sedative-hypnotics are designed to go a little further. They are used to both calm us down and induce physical rest or more commonly, sleep.

Just for the record I'm going to list a few "downers" so we can get a picture of how serious the use of them is in our culture. Old-timers include the infamous barbiturates Seconal and Tuinal; these have mostly been discarded from use today. More recent legal and similar drugs include Placidyl, Quaalude and Halcion. Some of the more potent "downers" include Thorazine, Mellaril and Prolixin. More widely used "downers" are Valium, Librium and the new favorite Xanax. I want to conclude with one product you may not think of as a "downer", it is Benadryl.

In my readings around this topic of "downers" I have discovered that they, as a classification of legal drugs, account for more than 1 billion prescriptions a year. I'm sure all of us can conclude that this widespread use of chemicals to take our emotional level from a difficult state to a more relaxed state says something. I much prefer to allow the reader to draw their own conclusions than to try to influence them, with one exception. It leaves me asking a question, why can't Americans deal with difficult emotions without resorting to drugs?

Of course there are other much used answers to becoming relaxed. Some of the additives we commonly use are food and alcohol. Do you remember my friend Jim from earlier in the chapter? He used ice cream as his "downer", and by the amount of ice cream consumed in our country, I don't think he is alone. Others simply like to eat enough volume of food so that their physiochemical processes kick in big time. Yes, they feel full, but there is more to it, they also physically slow down, and hence feel a little more relaxed. Haven't you ever eaten enough at lunch that you feel a nap might do you some good?

Instead of eating a big burger and fries, some of us choose to drink a beer or have a cocktail. Haven't we all either said or heard it said something like this, "I'm going to have a beer to unwind." This is because we know that the alcohol will help loosen us up emotionally. Alcohol is a commonly accepted "downer", and like all "downers" we can get to the point where we become emotionally dependent on alcohol to help deal with the difficult emotions found in our daily lives. When our compulsion to drink alcohol becomes a necessity, we have become trapped in an addiction, the emotional prison of alcoholism.

I have left this little piece of "downer" discussion until now because it really irritates me. Maybe I need a 'downer" before I write about it! What irritates me is the giving of the "downer" Ritalin to our children. We are doing so much damage to them that it breaks my heart. Ritalin is actually a stimulant in its biochemical nature, and it is a close chemical cousin to cocaine. It has an ability to help hyperactive children focus better, and was originally used mostly for that purpose. In today's culture it has become the drug used to treat any child that has emotional ups and downs.

The inevitable byproduct of this insanity of giving kids such powerful drugs is to create kids who will have a propensity to take drugs later. After all, aren't we giving them a cocaine cousin? Can you see why this irritates me? Instead of helping our children cope with life's ups and downs, we dose them up for the convenience of ourselves as parents and teachers. We put them on a path to chemical dependence; we point them toward an emotional prison. If you are one of those parents, please consider reviewing the need for this type of drug. Take the high road and help your child get away from this madness.

Boosting Our Emotional Performance

Earlier in the chapter I compared the use of special additives for refinery products with our use of chemical additives for altering of performance. Boosting performance was the last of these comparisons, and I spoke of it as making things run smoother, faster, hotter and more efficiently for refinery products such as gasoline or jet fuel. We can think of the Soul's emotional output in much the same way. We want to improve the emotions of the Soul. We might want to feel better, or have more energy, or perhaps feel more restful, maybe we might like to feel less stress. Emotions are one of the outputs of our Souls, and it is common to want to boost our personal emotional performance.

Can we measure emotional performance? With refinery products we can specifically define performance; we can measure it, test it, certify it and be specific on what it might be. Emotional performance is not that way. There is no way I can measure how much anger I might be experiencing as a response to a given situation. Also, if the same situation came up next week, would I have the same exact amount of anger? Probably not! Equally as important as being unable to objectively measure our own emotional performance, there is also no way an outside observer, like a social scientist, can objectively measure the change in someone's emotional state or performance. This is why we can say that emotional performance is purely an internally generated and observed subjective determination.

Putting this into plain language, only the person who is experiencing the changes in emotional performance can say what and how much of a change is occurring. From the outside we can watch the behavior of a person taking additives and make educated guesses about emotional performance. We can even quiz them and try to find out what the person taking the additives is experiencing. However, if you've ever talked to a person who has been drinking alcohol, you've probably heard them say they were perfectly fine to drive home. The question is simple, can you trust a person on additives to tell you accurately what their emotional changes might be. The answer is no.

I have said all this so that I might get to this point. A person who takes additives to improve their emotional performance is doing so for their own self-centered reasons. This person also doesn't really know if taking the additive is actually doing the job, meaning improving emotional performance. In fact they are basically experimenting on themselves in what a scientist would call "trial and error." They will try something and see if it gets them where they want to be. If it doesn't, they might try more of the same thing or try something different. If it does, they have found something that helps them deal with the emotional inadequacy they believe they have.

When we put these factors of the internal nature of emotional performance determination, the subjectiveness and the experimentation together, we create an understanding of this issue. Some people choose to use additives to change their emotional performance. Whether the additive works or not and the extent of its success is determined by the individual. Once a person has had some success modifying their feelings with an additive, they then acquire the knowledge that, for them, taking "something" helps. This, of course, puts them on the road to taking an additive of some kind every time they want to change their feelings. This is a trap!

The trap is this. Achieving success in improving emotional performance using additives leads to changes inside a person's Soul. The individual taking additives for improving emotional performance begins to change what their values, beliefs and attitudes (characteristics of the Heart) are towards dealing with what life brings. Prior to taking additives a person has certain values, beliefs and attitudes that he or she applies to handling the emotions of daily life. Once they have discovered that they can handle them by popping a pill, taking a drink or eating chocolate cake, these Heart characteristics will change.

As an example, let us consider the man who has had a hard day at work, with his boss riding him about something all day. Early on in his working life he might come home and tell his wife about it, and that worked to de-stress him, to the point that he was able to release or resolve his emotions. Then one day he chose to grab a beer as well, discovering that it seemed to help soothe his troubles away. In fact, he finds out that two beers are actually better than one for this, he gets over the situation more quickly and enjoys the evening more. He comes to believe that drinking a couple of beers helps him in dealing with the troubles that life always brings. Eventually he might get to the point where he reaches for a beer as a habit, not because he is troubled.

This was how a person I knew; we'll call him Joe, ended up becoming an alcoholic. He worked in a machine shop and was a bit of a perfectionist, which made him a little slower than his co-workers. His output quantity was not as high as the company wanted, and his boss seemed to always be on his case. In his mid twenties he says he began to unwind with a couple of beers but before long he was up to a six-pack every evening. He often ended up falling asleep in the recliner. At first his wife left him there, then his wife simply left him. He lost his family and ended up losing his job.

Joe had come to believe that having a couple of beers was actually an acceptable way of dealing with all the emotional hardships of life. It was only after he lost his wife and kids that he began to see things differently. He managed to get a new job and joined Alcoholics Anonymous; the people there have helped him get through the first phase of his recovery, stopping the drinking. The second phase is proving to be more difficult, working through the twelve steps, but at least he is working on it.

There are literally millions of men and women like my acquaintance Joe out there. There is no part of our culture which is not affected by the chase for emotional performance through using additives. In fact we have businesses that thrive on our desire to achieve some form of emotional performance enhancement through putting something into our biochemical system. I'll name a few: the illegal drug trade, the legal drug industry through the misuse of legal drugs, the soft drink business, the alcohol industry and my favorite the "Happy Hour" business. These are all businesses based on our individual desires to improve how we feel. I know this statement will challenge our understanding, so I'm going to ask this question. Does any person need any of the things I've listed to live?

I think it might also be helpful to list a few of the situations I've personally encountered that demonstrate how widespread this "chase for emotional performance" actually is. Let's see if you can relate to some of these people:

- The 50 something housewife who had a cocktail or two before her husband came home from work.
- The car mechanic who smoked a little weed each day at lunchtime, and drank beer every evening.
- The telephone company executive who always seemed to be carrying a cola in his hand.
- The plain 30 something woman who kept a supply of chocolate in her purse "for stressful times."
- The ex gang member who used to snort cocaine with his friends, who are now all dead.
- The high school athlete who took steroids to get on the team, and continued to take them after he left college.
- The truck driver who used to smoke weed while he was on the road to relieve his boredom.
- The hotel manager who used to binge eat and then take laxatives to try to stay thin.

As you can see from this short list there are a myriad of people and reasons to take additives for emotional performance. In each of these examples we can see that the underlying reason for choosing to take additives was to deal with personal emotions. For all these people it seemed to work, until they couldn't deal with daily life without them. So many of us turn to some chemical method of dealing with difficult emotions. This is when our own emotions are controlling our life. Using additives helps until we cannot cope without them. That is when they, the additives, are in control of our emotions, and that is when they have become an emotional prison.

Additives and SPAR

Now it is time to turn to looking at this whole issue of taking additives using the SPAR analytical approach discussed earlier in the first book.

As I've said in prior chapters, there is usually one dominant SPAR factor at work within the falling into and staying in an emotional prison, although all four can contribute. In this case of the additive prison it seems that the "Performance" and "Responsibility" factors may be more significant.

Starting with "Security", we must remember that the basic issue here is our answer to the important question, "How do I feel about myself?" The person who generally feels negatively toward themselves has many choices on how to deal with this Soul problem. One of these is additives.

Having a negative feeling toward oneself can be very debilitating. Having a sense of inadequacy or worthlessness seems to drag us down and sometimes stop us from functioning well. Some of us discover the apparent benefit of additives in seemingly making this set of feelings go away. We as a society use a whole range of additives to deal with this problem.

Tom, a man I worked with many years ago, used to walk around with a cup of black coffee, because it seemed to make him feel better in the mornings. The problem was that Tom drank coffee all day, and probably drank as much as three pots every day. One co-worker used to keep a supply of chocolate in her desk drawer, "for when things aren't going well." I worked with one young man who used to ingest cocaine every morning to get himself up for his day. I'm guessing that any person who reads this will be able to identify people they know who take additives to feel better about themselves.

So instead of taking what might be a harder road in trying to understand how we feel about ourselves and resolving the relevant emotions, we try to change them. This is like putting a band-aid over an infected wound. When we do that the wound isn't visible any more, but it is still there. Most of us would not do that with a physical wound, but some of us will do that with a Soul wound by taking an additive to cover it up emotionally. Of course the cover up done through taking additives doesn't actually deal with the problem, but it does provide temporary relief from any emotional pain we have due to feelings of insecurity. Sometimes just getting drunk and going emotionally numb seems to be better than feeling useless about oneself.

Deep-seated feelings of insecurity can certainly be self treated this way by taking additives, but they will not be resolved or even diminished by the taking of substances. It is far more likely that a person will, within their Soul, come to a new understanding of themselves that will be worse than where they started. Let me explain.

Once an individual taking additives to cover up their feelings of personal insecurity realizes that they are not working, a new thought, an awareness, grows inside of them. On top of believing that they aren't worthy or some other negative assessment of themselves, they start to believe that the taking of additives proves something new. What is new is that their original negativity wasn't accurate, and in fact they are even less worthy than they thought and have been proving that by using something. This can be thought of as a spiral downwards where a user feels more and more negative about themselves. They try harder and harder to make the additives work believing that they will help. As we all know, it never does, and it is a fool's quest, which results in some cases in death, but mostly in broken people.

I will acknowledge that some people are helped in their personal insecurity by the medical profession through the strategic use of legal drugs. The problem is that often this is a cop-out. This is because either the individual is not willing to do the hard work of seeking emotional healing or the doctors are taking the easy way out. Legal drugs can often be the temporary fix that turns into a long-term solution, but doesn't ever get to the root causes of insecurity. This of course is the great dilemma of the psychiatric profession, combining drugs and psychology to the permanent solving of a person's emotional troubles.

If we recall the three emotional objectives we discussed earlier, we can see that a person trying to deal with personal insecurity might be taking additives to achieve any one or even all of the three. My personal choice for the most prevalent objective would be the second, which is, stabilize our emotional state. This is because the struggle with feeling okay with oneself is largely an issue of coming to terms with ones emotions.

The taking of additives to deal with personal insecurity is simply not an adequate solution to the inherent problem of feeling negatively toward oneself. It is really not a solution at all, and when I deal with healing later in the next book, we will see better ways of handling this. At this point we just need to acknowledge that additives can trap a person who feels insecure, offering false hope, and delivering an individual to an emotional prison.

I want to move on to considering the SPAR factor of "Performance. The basic question here is "How do I feel about myself, due to what I do?" We ought to ask ourselves if a person struggles with that question, can they seemingly benefit from taking additives? The clear answer is obviously, yes!

One of the core misunderstandings of the human race is equating what we do with who we are. How often do you hear something spoken like this, "I am a bricklayer", or "I am a schoolteacher?" They are statements made in response to a question like, "What do you do for a living?" Our response is made by identifying the activity of work or what we do, with who we are. This, of course, can lead us to thinking negatively about ourselves when our performance is not up our own perceived standards of acceptability. So now let us look at this misunderstanding of "self" and how it might affect someone in the context of additives.

Have you ever failed a test? Most of us have, and I would guess all of us feel "bummed out" about it to some level. We might feel disappointed, we might feel angry, we might even be in denial about our negative feelings by saying "I really don't care about the result." The question we actually must ask is "What do we do with these feelings?" Some of us simply resolve the feelings and move on. Others don't do this. These are the people who are affected by the SPAR factor of performance, and some of them turn to additives for help.

One of the classic examples of this is the cheating athlete. How many times have we heard of an athlete turning to steroids for help with performance? This is a problem all the way from middle school to the top of the sports professions. The great denial is that they all do it to "enhance physical performance." This is an argument of misdirection and needs to be refuted. They actually all do it to feel better about themselves. Consider the baseball player who takes steroids so he can bulk up and hit more home runs. Is he really doing it to improve physical performance? No, he is doing it so he can feel better about his physical performance, and thereby feel better about himself.

If we sit and think about it we can probably all come up with examples of people we know who take additives to help with the "feelings due to performance" problem. How about a judge who succumbs to cocaine after getting frustrated about not being able to lock up criminals when they are so obviously guilty. And how about the actress who turns to alcohol each evening as she fails to get the roles she wants. And the girl down the street who binges on food, and then throws it all up later because she doesn't feel thin enough. There are so many of these types of scenarios being played out every day where additives are taken to deal with the feelings that arise from self-perceptions of low performance. Look closely and you will see them.

Let's go back to the beginning of the chapter where we listed the three emotional objectives in taking additives. It is relatively easy to see that a person like the cheating athlete is trying to boost their emotional state (the third emotional objective) by taking something. Any person who takes an additive to help them deal with the problem of negative feelings about him or herself due to performance runs a risk. The risk is that they will become dependent on the additives to get through life. We call that an addiction, and it is an emotional prison.

The third SPAR factor is "Acceptance", where we address the enormous question, "How do I feel about myself, due to my perception of how others feel and think about me?" If you've got this far in the book you probably realize that I think this SPAR factor may be the most significant of all four of them. As I write this I am wondering just how many prescriptions are filled each year due to the feelings that go with this.

I said in an earlier chapter that when acceptance from others is a big emotional issue, you are basically handing over power and control to them. Well, with additives we make this problem bigger. Let's go through what happens in a typical scenario.

When a person has to have the acceptance of others to feel good about themselves, they get locked into a pattern of life that will always end up in negative feelings. I use the word "always" here because unless a person deals with the problem of needing acceptance from others this pattern will certainly happen. The pattern is this; they will generally find a way to gain acceptance from every person who is of importance to them. However, there will always be a significant individual in their life who will not be accepting of them in the eyes of the person needing acceptance. This may be either a real or a perceived non-acceptance.

Even if the person needing acceptance had several hundred close personal contacts and only one wouldn't give acceptance, this would be a problem. This problem, with its accompanying negative emotions, is so strong that it can lead even to murder. Consider all the tyrants that have existed - what do they do to people that disagree with them? They have them killed because disagreement to a tyrant equals non-acceptance or disapproval. Never underestimate the power of disapproval or non-acceptance in a person's life.

Fortunately most people who need significant acceptance aren't tyrants, but they still have the difficulty inside their Soul of unresolved negative feelings about themselves. So, how do they deal with this? Some turn to work, or religion or some other way of masking the problem, but some of them turn to additives. Additives are a convenient way of relieving oneself of the burden of internal negativity that can come with not feeling accepted even by only one person.

It is all too easy to turn to our doctor and say, I'm depressed, can you help me? We get a prescription and pill-by-pill we achieve our emotional objectives of first stability and maintaining those improved feeelings. Some of us may turn to the bottle and find that a couple of gin and tonics seems to soothe us. Whatever our additive may be, the truth is that it doesn't really help, it makes things worse by adding to our problems.

We start with the problem of having to deal with negative emotions which come with a Soul that believes it needs acceptance from others, like we all need air or water. Then we add the dependence on additives to it. It is as if we are determined to fall into the prison of needing acceptance and then we add a doubly thick wall around ourselves by getting addicted to something. Looking at a person in this emotional prison, we would probably only see the additive problem unless we investigated further.

The final SPAR factor is Responsibility, where we deal with the nagging problem of how we feel about ourselves due to our ability to meet certain standards. Often, when we can't do things to the standard we have set for ourselves, we experience negative emotions such as a sense of inadequacy. Just as we find with the other SPAR factors, additives can be an answer, although not a healthy answer, to dealing with these emotions.

I'm just going to offer a simple example here. How many times do we hear of professional athletes or other performers having a substance problem? What does a performer do when they start to realize they are not able to meet their own subjective standards? Some of them work harder, some retire, and some take additives. I often wonder how many famous people end up with drinking problems or a drug addiction after they fade from the limelight.

It is always the same story; some of us try to deal with our negative feelings by using a chemical of some kind. And it is always a trap waiting to be sprung. When it is sprung, we become prisoners of the very thing we thought would help, the additive.

In conclusion I want to acknowledge that the emotional prison of additives is definitely different from all the other prisons in one respect. It has the added complication of having a physical component. This makes the taking of additives to meet emotional objectives doubly damaging to an individual.

We all must remember that a person who uses food or drugs or alcohol to the point they are trapped is dealing with a set of underlying psychological issues. Simply stopping the behavior doesn't change the problem, and that is why rehab fails so often, it doesn't actually get to the root emotional difficulty.

A Spiritual Perspective

I don't think we can finish this subject without addressing what God might think about the misuse of additives. I don't plan to speak for Him, but as a Bible teacher I would be remiss if I didn't point out what needs to be said. There is a Scripture that has a lot of relevance here:

1 Cor 6:19-20 - Or do you not know that your body is a temple of the Holy Spirit who is in you, whom you have from God, and that you are not your own? For you have been bought with a price: therefore glorify God in your body.

For the non-Christian this message from God is nonsensical, but for the believer it is a direct command. The context of these two verses is that they are part of a larger section of Scripture that deals with using the body in immoral ways. This includes the misuse of additives!

This Scripture quite rightly points out that our bodies, which contain our Souls, are the dwelling place of the Holy Spirit. It then points out that we were bought with a price, meaning Jesus paid the price for our immoral behavior, which we call sin, through His death. God then tells us that because of this fact, we are to glorify Him in our bodies.

The big question for all of us is therefore this, "When we use additives are we glorifying God?" Each person must address this for himself or herself, remembering that we will all have to account for how we treat our own bodies in some way in our future. For me, this is a matter of obedience or disobedience to God's instruction.

17

VICTIMHOOD

*The ideal tyranny is that which is ignorantly self-administered by its
victims. The most perfect slaves are, therefore, those which blissfully
and unawaredly enslave themselves.*
Dresden James

This chapter is going to be about an emotional prison that may not at first
appear to be one. It is about "victimhood." There are so many "victims"
in this world, and we are going to talk about some of them. To start
though I want to discuss the world's first person that exhibited
victimhood. We find him, in the beginning, in Genesis:

*Gen 4:13-14 - Cain said to the Lord, "My punishment is too great to
bear! "Behold, You have driven me this day from the face of the
ground; and from Your face I will be hidden, and I will be a vagrant
and a wanderer on the earth, and whoever finds me will kill me.*

The story is this. Adam and Eve had a son, his name was Cain, then they
had another, he was called Abel. After they grew old enough to be
accountable for their actions they both brought offerings to the Lord
God. Cain's offering was not what God required, and was not thought
well of, but Abel's offering was. Cain became resentful toward his
brother and toward God, and subsequently murdered Abel. After God
confronted Cain and asked him where his brother was, Cain uttered these
famous words. "I do not know. Am I my brother's keeper?"

As a result of Cain's choices to murder his brother, then lie about it to
God, he received a just consequence for his actions. This is where Cain
paints himself as a victim as shown in our two verses above. He
basically tells God that the punishment is too much, and that he will be a
destitute bum and someone will kill him. Cain's brother was the actual
murder victim, but Cain twists it all around as if he is the victim with his,
woe is me, statement. Cain has entered what I am going to label a "Soul
state" of victimhood. Let's now define what that is.

Victimhood is an internal condition of a person's Soul where they are feeling the negative emotions of suffering due to real or perceived action or actions against them. We can see from this definition that victimhood revolves around negative emotions, and this can set up a person to moving toward becoming trapped in an emotional prison.

Now we have defined victimhood let's return to the story of Cain and pick it apart a little more. It is important to understand that Cain's murder of his own little brother and the subsequent lie to God about what he had done were the result of the workings of his Soul. If we look at the facts of what happened and see Cain's responses, we will gain some insight into some of the elements of how victimhood develops.

First, we should note that God had instructed Cain and Abel in the bringing of offerings. The Bible is consistent throughout on this issue, it is to be the first part of whatever you have or gain or earn. It is apparent that they knew this because Abel did indeed bring the first part as instructed, and it was acceptable to God. Cain did not do this, he did bring an offering, but it was what he chose, and it was not what he was told to do. His response to the instructions, which was disobedience, was the source of the rest of his troubles, and was why he ended up in victimhood.

This is the disobedience that Cain exhibited. He knew that he was to bring the first part of his harvest since he was a farmer. God has established this as a method of humans reminding themselves that all things are God's in the sense of ownership and that all income, whether harvests, new flocks of sheep or paychecks are ours only through his provision. The offering was a way of saying "thank you" to Him, and was for the benefit of the offeree, not for the benefit of God, as He needs nothing. Cain evidently did not appreciate this and he chose to violate God's simple instruction, and God was gracious enough to call him out on it. In fact God was so gracious that he gave him a personal warning and a conditional promise. Let us see what God said after the offering incident:

Gen 4:6-7 - Then the Lord said to Cain, "Why are you angry? And why has your countenance fallen?" If you do well, will not your countenance be lifted up? And if you do not do well, sin is crouching at the door; and its desire is for you, but you must master it."

Cain was angry, the Scripture doesn't say exactly why, and God knew this and still gave him a way out. He basically told him that he could get back on track and things would get better for him. However, if he didn't then "sin was crouching at his door" and it would overtake him and become his master. Let's now see how the "Soul state" of victimhood developed in Cain, and apply it to our modern lives.

Deep inside the Soul of Cain we can see a few things. The first is that in his Mind he knew what the instruction was from his authority figure, God. It was to bring an acceptable offering. The second thing we see, and we have to infer this, is that he believed in his Heart that he could substitute a lesser offering. Right there we have a Soul conflict, what he knows and what he believes are not the same thing. When the situation gets to the point where it is time to make the offering, the conflict gets resolved by his Will. Cain's Will makes a choice, and the choice is to oppose what God had said to do, and do what he wanted for his own self-centered reasons. We call this rebellion. In Cain's situation rebellion led to his refusal to obey his authority figure, God, which we call disobedience.

At some point in this story something very significant happened inside the Soul of Cain. I personally believe it happened at the moment he chose to rebel against God. The attitude of Cain's Heart changed from at least a passive acceptance of God's authority to active rebelliousness and opposition to His authority. The Bible calls attitude the "inclination" of the Heart. So Cain's Heart began to incline toward rebelliousness. For Cain this meant that he was not going to be disposed to accepting God or His direction in his life. In fact while he, Cain, was probably going to comply if forced by God in something, his Heart's attitude would not. This meant that he would always be "inclined" to do something different to what God, and most likely any authority figure, would tell him needed to be done.

As often happens, disobedience is followed by exposure of the willful rebellion by the authority figure, and God deemed Cain's offering unacceptable. God made an interesting choice of His own, He chose to not punish Cain or force him to comply with the instruction. Instead God chose to be gracious. He gave Cain an opportunity to come clean by asking him why he was angry, and why he was feeling down. God then warns Cain the result of not doing the right thing, which would have been to choose to obey, which our Scripture, in this case, calls "doing well." God tells Cain that sin is about to overtake him, unless he masters it. In his rebelliousness Cain took the wrong path and murdered his little brother.

God, even though He knew everything that had transpired, did an amazing thing; He gave Cain a chance to confess. This is where we see Cain utter that infamous statement of denial of responsibility, "Am I my brother's keeper." So we can see yet another attitude enter the picture we are painting of Cain's Heart, denial. In Cain's case, this attitude is so strong that it enables him to overcome any sense of right and wrong, and of real guilt he might be feeling.

At this point God then chooses to give Cain a consequence for his actions of murdering Abel and lying about it. God tells him that the earth will no longer yield to him so that he cannot continue to be a farmer, and that he will become a vagrant and a wanderer. This is where the whining begins and the victimhood appears in its fullness.

In his emotion of anger Cain's attitude of rebellion was further twisted into a desire to strike out, and he struck out against the only person possible, his own little brother. I can't say for sure but it looks like Cain was trying to get back at God for some reason. We call this revenge. Revenge is another new attitude of the Heart in our story. Cain is thinking of himself as a victim, and he is actually and openly suffering the natural result of his original disobedience. Our verses called this a "fallen countenance", indicating that he was appearing downcast. We now come to the point where he is downcast, he has murdered his little brother, he has lied about it, and he has been given his consequence. All through this process his Heart's attitude has been deteriorating, first it was an attitude of compliance, then rebelliousness, then revenge, then denial and now two new attitudes appear, blame and helplessness. To see these we need to look at Cain's reaction to God's informing him of the consequence. Look back a few paragraphs to Gen 4:13-14, which I previously quoted.

I can imagine that Cain was pointing his index finger at God while he was saying, "You have driven me away, and you have given me too much of a consequence." He seems to have forgotten that he has committed murder; instead he blames God because life has suddenly become tougher for him. Then to finish his short discourse, Cain sinks into his "woe is me" state by making his declaration of hopelessness. I'll paraphrase it here, "I'm going to become a homeless person and somebody will probably kill me."

108

When I'm trying to figure out why someone behaves the way they do I like to ask the question, "What is going on inside their Soul?" So, what is going on inside Cain's Soul? This is a picture of a conflicted Soul, a Soul where the Mind, Heart and Will are not in unity or harmony with each other. Let's lay out some of the things we can see.

In the Mind, where the characteristics of knowledge, understanding and wisdom reside, we can that Cain knows and understands what the right offering was and that murdering his little brother was wrong. His ability to apply wisdom seems to be lacking. In the Heart, where his values, beliefs and attitudes are located, things were dark. We have seen how he didn't believe he needed to obey God. Mostly we have seen attitudes of compliance, rebelliousness, denial and revenge. These things also seem to indicate that he placed more value on his own self-centered desires than on his relationship with God.

The conflict within the Soul of Cain was therefore between his knowing what the right things to do were, and the state of his Heart, which was one of "self." By "self" I mean that very human set of values, beliefs, and attitudes that say "We are more important than anybody else." In Cain, just as in all of us, the Will has to sort things out. It appears that within Cain the Heart dominated, and the Will chose to commit murder and lie.

As Cain received his consequence, we see two new attitudes begin to appear in his Heart; blame and hopelessness. Blame comes as a result of his not being able to accept the truth that he was personally responsible for all that happened. So he blamed God for the consequence, completely stuffing and ignoring the facts about why he received the consequence or punishment. He also felt the feelings of powerlessness that came when he actually realized that he had no control over the situation. Like a lot of us today, this sense of powerlessness was followed by a sense of helplessness. This helplessness then became part of the attitudes of Cain's Heart, as he took the feeling of helplessness and made it a permanent part of his Soul characteristics. The combination of blame and helplessness produced in Cain a state of victimhood.

Right there you have it! Attitudes of blame and helplessness are at the root of the emotional prison of victimhood. Let's look at how this might play out in a person's life.

No matter how they get there (which I will talk about below) when attitudes of blame and hopelessness are present in a Soul, the person involved will be chained down by victimhood. The situation is this; an individual carries the attitudes of blame and helplessness in their Soul. They then experience life's normal flow, and circumstances arise. They apply their attitudes of blame and helplessness within their Soul, which produces thoughts and more importantly, emotions. This is the predominant thought; "I am not to blame", and of course this means that somebody else is responsible. The next thought is something like this; "I can't help myself in this situation."

The emotions that come into the everyday life of a person struggling with victimhood are very debilitating. They experience feelings like powerlessness, inadequacy, incompetence and frustration. These in turn lead to pain, shame and often anger. These feelings are feelings that often can control a person. This is where we need to distinguish two groups of victims, those that choose to stay victims and those that don't.

Every person experiences the events, situations or circumstances that make them a victim. Every person then experiences the kind of emotions that I described above. A person who allows those feelings to control his or her actions is in victimhood; a person who does not is free from it. The person who stays with those feelings stays a victim, the person who chooses to overcome them does not. It is the way a person chooses to deal with their feelings which determines if they live life as a victim or if they experience a life having freedom from this prison.

Observations on the Origins of Victimhood

The actual origin of the emotional prison of victimhood is of course how a person responds to the negative emotions generated within their Soul when they perceive themselves to be a victim. This is not dependent on whether they actually are a victim, only if they believe themselves to be one. In the previous segment we identified Cain as a person exhibiting victimhood, and it was all due to his own thoughts, feelings and actions. This meant that he was suffering due to his own activities and not because of another person's actions. That meant that he was not even a victim. He had all the negative emotions that were a result of his applying his attitudes of blame and hopelessness within his Soul, and he chose victimhood.

What I really want to talk about here is not the actual core reason we might choose to step into victimhood, but other factors that influence us as a culture in this problematical prison. To do this I'm going to use an example from recent history. I live near the gulf coast, where we live through hurricane season each year. On August 29th 2005, the eye of Hurricane Katrina crossed over New Orleans. This event demonstrated many aspects of how victimhood is manifested in our society.

Let us be sure to understand and acknowledge things about Hurricane Katrina. It wasn't a very powerful storm, but it was big and did truly significant damage. It is the most costly, in dollar terms, storm ever to hit the US, and the latest estimate I could find was that it caused between $80 and $85 dollars worth of property damage in 2005 dollars. Worse than that, it was one of the five most costly in terms of lives lost. It is believed that at least 1836 people lost their lives as a direct result of the storm. Eighty percent of New Orleans was flooded, and a lot of it is still not rebuilt. In fact, four years later some residents of that city were still living in trailers around the country. It completely decimated the city's economy and there were many victims.

Human behavior seemed to be at its best and worst during this time. I witnessed many examples of people helping people. I also witnessed many people, particularly governmental types, acting with complete irresponsibility and in self-serving ways. I saw blame being thrown around as most people who were in the public eye attempted to avoid being held accountable for their poor performance. It seems to me that the only organizations which performed well were the churches and other non-governmental entities that provided for people's needs as soon as humanly possible.

The most striking thing for me was the actions of countless individuals who chose to act out of their emotional state created by their attitudes of hopelessness and blame. There was an air of paralysis, of inability or desire to act to get out of the way of the storm. I wonder how many of the 1836 lost lives were due to decisions driven by victimhood, due to attitudes of hopelessness and expectations that someone else is responsible for taking care of them. I want to look at why this was so prevalent in New Orleans, and contrast it with other communities who were equally devastated, but didn't act out.

To do this contrast we must first remind ourselves of some basic things about the Soul that were discussed in earlier chapters. If you recall, we talked about how values, beliefs and attitudes are formed in us as children. We open up the gateway of our Will and let in information from those who are close to us. Primarily this will be parents, although other family members, neighbors, the general community and the media are all significant influences. In this way we pass on family and community values, beliefs, and attitudes, whether they are healthy or not.

When we look what the response to the impending hurricane and its disastrous consequences were, we can see a distinct difference between the New Orleans area and the Mississippi gulf coast community. Both groups had flooding, destroyed homes, washed out roads and displaced populations. The big differences become visible when we see the actions of the people both before and after the storm.

In the New Orleans area there was a reluctance to leave, a reluctance to evacuate the population, as well as an inept government from city to state. Most incredible was the reluctance to ask the federal government for assistance until the storm was right on top of the community, when it was too late for help. Commentators suggested the possibility that this was due to the stupidity of the leaders which was derived from their self-centeredness, but this is not a good analysis. The problem of ineptitude and paralysis was the byproduct of the irresponsible attitudes of blame and hopelessness; it was the result of victimhood. This inability to act in the interests of the people because of victimhood resulted in deaths and ruined lives. Victimhood claimed its own victims!

Compare New Orleans with the gulf coast of Mississippi. The leaders uniformly issued early and strong evacuations. People got out andthere was only minor loss of life. There was no paralysis; there was healthy and decisive action. The characteristic of victimhood was not seen at work in the communal aspects of dealing with this storm.

After Katrina passed, the differences were even more evident. In New Orleans it was the dead bodies, the out of control crime, and the wasted city resources that were obvious. Watching the interviews of the survivors you can see and hear "why didn't anyone come to save me" and the "I'm waiting for you to rescue me" attitudes. The finger pointing of the leadership as they all tried to cover their rear ends, and the dishonesty about their role in making this worse than it had to be showed us both the attitudes of blame and hopelessness. It was more natural (meaning normal to them) to blame others than to admit their own lack of competence and failure. It was also natural for those same leaders to say things like "What could we do", a statement of hopelessness. I was truly disgusted by what I witnessed.

Now, compare that to what we saw from the state of Mississippi. They had declared their "state of emergency" early and once the appropriate authorities had cleared the area for return, they got on with rebuilding. There was almost no whining and complaining. As a community they wisely accepted the federal emergency money and started to use it to rebuild. They didn't sit and wallow in their misery, and they didn't let their losses stop them from moving forward in recapturing their lives.

This comparison brings to mind a very accurate Scripture verse that simply says it all, and I'm going to use the old King James Version as it says it so well:

Prov 29:18 - Where there is no vision, the people perish. KJV

The attitudes of blame and hopelessness combined in New Orleans to clearly demonstrate the lack of vision of the leaders. The result was that some people perished needlessly.

How did this happen? Why did the city of New Orleans and its people suffer more than they needed to? Why did so many of them perish?

It is easy for me to point out the obvious lack of quality leadership involved, but I don't really think that is the true problem. I think it goes deeper; it goes to the culture of victimhood so prevalent in the city. I cannot even guess when it developed, but it did. Living in victimhood as a lifestyle did not just happen; it begins with one or two people, or maybe even a few. These are people with Souls that carry the attitudes of blame and hopelessness. These people somehow survive and in their own eyes prosper, meaning they do well by their own standards. They pass on the attitudes of blame and hopelessness to their children, and to their family and neighbors. The children are particularly vulnerable as the gateways of their Souls are constantly open to the input of the parents. The children grow up living out a life of victimhood. They grow up with victimhood as a generational curse; they grow up in it as an emotional prison.

With this emotional prison being collectively experienced a new social situation develops, a new culture, a culture of victimhood.

Culture of Victimhood

Although I have singled out New Orleans as an example, we can also see this culture of victimhood with its very obvious attitudes, blame and hopelessness, in other places both in the US and around the world. This culture of victimhood is extremely dangerous as it leads to several levels of problems.

The first problem level is in the personal or individual life. A person in the emotional prison of victimhood has a normal response to most of the situations they get into. The response comes out of their attitudes of blame and hopelessness. For an individual in this emotional prison everything bad that happens is someone else's fault. Our regular prisons are full of people who want to blame others for their own actions. When a person lives with the attitude of hopelessness he or she finds it easy to say within their Soul, "I can't do any better, life is hopeless." This person will not try to improve life. If they do they may not try very hard, and if they fail they tend to give up easily, going back to the belief that everything is hopeless. The life of an individual living out their attitudes of blame and hopelessness tends to be a self-perpetuating life.

Next, we move to the extended family level. The attitudes of blame and hopelessness run through this mini-culture. They are reinforced constantly as if each member is justifying their position of victimhood to each other. Whenever a person is actually able to get out of the extended family environment it is not celebrated as a release from a prison. It is viewed as selling out or becoming a traitor. The family that lives in victimhood does all it can to keep its members that way. This control is best understood as a family survival method. When a person does get out and experiences how life can be outside the prison, they do not want to go back. For this person, the family often becomes a nest of vipers, full of poisonous people, not poisonous out of maliciousness, but out of survival. Once a person gets out of this prison, they try to stay away from then on.

The third level is the neighborhood or community. The old saying, "Birds of a feather flock together" seems to fit well here. People tend to both associate with and physically live near others who have similar values, beliefs and attitudes. This is true all over the world. So when we see a collection of people together who have the attitudes of blame and hopelessness, we have a neighborhood of victimhood. This can be a miserable place.

The neighborhood of victimhood is subject to all kinds of problems. The community is made up of people whose first response to anything is one of blame and hopelessness. When things aren't going well, it is someone else's fault or responsibility, so people won't step up and take care of normal community issues. When a sense of hopelessness is present, individuals are going to have the attitude that they can't change or improve their everyday life, and maybe nobody from outside can either. This leaves the neighborhood open to unscrupulous community organizers who will use the attitudes of victimhood for their own self-centered purposes. It also opens the door to crime, because the victims won't act to defend themselves due to their sense of hopelessness. The last big problem would be substance abuse. Drugs will almost always be found in a neighborhood of victimhood, because drugs provide at least a short-term fix for the negative feelings that trap a person in victimhood.

The fourth level to look at is the town or city, and this is where things get a little fuzzy. If the pockets of neighborhoods of victimhood are sufficiently large enough, they will begin to exercise political power through the ballot box or some other political mechanism. In the case of a democracy, the people who are trapped by victimhood will elect any person who identifies with their situation and promises to fix it. For the record, no politician can ever fix it, because it is a Soul problem that can only be dealt with at the personal level. The problem with this is that the people elected or otherwise placed in power at the local government level through a "victimhood vote" tend to be users. They often turn out to be personally corrupt, and they use the real or perceived victim status of others for their own purposes. A high level of victimhood in the population will make them vulnerable to corrupt, self-serving leadership.

The last level to look at is the state or nation. Here we see much the same situation as the previous level in terms of politics or governmental leadership. The major difference here is that the corruption may not just be about money, it may also be about power and control. In fact this is the root of revolution. If you look at all the successful (in the sense of changing of political power) major popular revolutions within nations over the last 100 years you see the same ingredients; a population which has a high incidence of victimhood and leaders who are power seekers. Examples are the Russian revolution under Lenin, the German revolution under Hitler, the Chinese revolution under Mao Tse Tung and the Cuban revolution under Castro. More recently we have seen the revolutions in Zimbabwe under Mugabe and Venezuela under Chavez. In each of these popular victimhood-driven changes of power, the people ended up being more oppressed or at least just as oppressed as they were before the revolt. This is because the revolution does not change the national character that is the composite of the values, beliefs and attitudes of the people. It does not change the Souls who are in the emotional prison of victimhood.

I've written about all these levels of problems as I've called them so that we can fully appreciate the power that victimhood has over people. It can literally lead to slavery, where the people voluntarily allow themselves to be under the control of others. There may not be whips and chains used in a city like New Orleans, but the people are still largely enslaved to the political system and its masters. The good news is this; there is hope!

One of the most interesting aspects of the Katrina disaster to me is this. So many of the displaced residents of New Orleans chose to not go back. This is because they were forced to evacuate through circumstance and found that life in a place like Baton Rouge, Dallas or Houston was better for them. The physical displacement allowed them to see that they could live a life of personal responsibility and hope. They could throw off the chains of blame and hopelessness. So many of them were finally free and there is no way they want to go back to the emotional prison of victimhood.

SPAR and Victimhood

Let's look at victimhood at the personal level through the SPAR analysis and see how it can develop in an individual.

The first SPAR factor is Security where we look at the question, 'How do I feel about myself?" For the person struggling with the feelings that result from always responding to situations with the attitudes of blame and hopelessness, this is a major problem.

There is a major tendency for an individual who feels insecure about themselves to think in "I" and "me" ways. Examples are; the hurricane happened to me, I failed to get a job, I am useless, the world owes me. In the case of someone carrying the attitudes of blame and hopelessness, it forces the thinking of this person into a "me only" box, with everything in life being about them. Let's look at why this might be so.

Back in my original discussion on the subject of personal security I noted that this factor is a dynamic factor. This is where all of us experience times of feeling more or occasionally less secure about who we are. Periodically we feel emotions of inadequacy or worthlessness or, as is relevant in this discussion, hopelessness. It is our response to these emotions which causes us to develop beliefs that we are not secure. The emotions seem to reinforce any low self-esteem we may be carrying around.

The person struggling with the two attitudes we have identified which accompany victimhood is constantly generating negative emotions that lead to insecurity. As they apply their attitude of blame to their life situations all they can see is that someone other than them is responsible for all the things that happen to them. This is the kind of person who rear-ends you at a red traffic light and tries to explain that it is your fault. I'm sure you've also met the person who fails a test because they haven't studied and declares the failure was due to the professor's questions. We have all met the blamers.

The blamers tell lies, similar to the two I mentioned above, in every part of their lives. In fact they do it so much and so often that they actually start to believe them. This leads to a sense of powerlessness and inability to deal with life, which we often call inadequacy. Can you imagine going through life believing that you can't do anything to improve your lot, because someone is always keeping you from getting ahead? Is it any surprise that a blamer ends up having a negative sense of self-worth?

Then there is the attitude of hopelessness. This is where a person goes into all of their life's situations with the confident expectation that things will go wrong or that they will fail. And of course they are proved correct, at least in their own eyes. This is the person who won't try to score well on a test, and manages to achieve exactly what their attitude leads to, a low score. Have you ever seen a kid not go for a catch in baseball, or pass the ball to a teammate on the basketball court when they have a shot? These are the type of actions that come out of a sense of hopelessness.

The feelings that arise from the frequent reinforcement of the sense of hopelessness are the same ones we have been talking about. Inadequacy, worthlessness and so on, these emotions lead to an understanding and a belief that because I can't do things well, I am less than others or I am nothing and nobody. With this lack of belief in themselves or a sense of personal value comes the sense of insecurity. The personal insecurity then reinforces the attitude of hopelessness as being a correct and proven one. The hopelessness and insecurity connection is a vicious cycle which pushes the individual into the emotional prison of victimhood.

The second SPAR factor is Performance. In this factor we look at the question, "How do I feel about myself, due to the things I do?" As one might expect the issue of failure and its results within the Soul of a person is a key factor for an individual who struggles with victimhood.

When the attitude of blame is present in the Heart of a person, they are always looking for another person or entity to point the finger at when things don't go well. It is very likely that the attitude of blame has been taught, as we discussed earlier, or acquired through the experience of dealing with performance shortfalls in which a person doesn't feel okay with what and how well they have been doing things in life. The negative emotions that come with a performance shortfall have to be dealt with somehow. Some people resolve them by working at doing life better; others figure out that emotional relief can come from blaming a person, or an organization like "the government", for real or perceived failures. Even if the attitude of blame is not learned it can therefore be acquired and reinforced through how we deal with the emotions that spring up within us when we fail.

Blamers therefore put themselves in a position to not take responsibility for how well they deal with life. As I have mentioned before I have wrestled with the issue of performance and fear of failure throughout my life. The origins of this go back to my early childhood abandonment. I could blame my parents for all the failures of my life if I wanted to, and that would a big lie. Most of my failures were due to my inability to deal with my emotions and make good choices. Others who have been abandoned will decide to blame their parents when they make bad behavioral choices as adults. It allows them to temporarily handle the emotional results of failure. These people get trapped in their thinking, and end up in the emotional prison of victimhood.

Now let's add the attitude of hopelessness into the picture. When a person carries this they are always inclined to think "failure" in life's everyday situations. It is very fatalistic in nature and makes it hard for a person to see success in any form. For example, I tried out for a semi-pro soccer team once, and I wasn't selected. If I had an attitude of hopelessness I might say that I failed and it was always going to be that way and I might give up soccer altogether. For those who don't carry this sense of hopelessness around this is hard to connect with. Why wouldn't I say, "I almost made it, I achieved to a really good level, I performed admirably?" The person without hope sees life differently. They would say, "I failed, I didn't perform well", and it is a short step in thinking to then say, "I am a failure."

The person carrying the attitude of hopelessness around doesn't succeed in doing life well, they experience all those negative emotions we have talked about. They are transferring their thoughts and feelings about not performing well into thoughts and feelings about not being adequate. This then becomes the basis for staying in a victim mode, and living in the emotional prison of victimhood.

Our third SPAR factor is Acceptance, where we ask, "How do I feel about myself, due to my perception of how others think and feel about me?"

In my opinion this is the least important of the four SPAR factors in looking at victims and victimhood, but it is an interesting subject to ponder. The victim really doesn't care what others are thinking and feeling about them while they are in a victimhood mode. This is because as a victim they are trying to get their needs met, and are totally self-absorbed. This leaves no room for consideration of what others think or feel about them. The example I run across almost every day is the homeless person. They just want money from me for their own purposes. They don't care what they look like, what they smell like or how they generally appear, they are trying to survive and seem decidedly beaten down.

When a person is in the emotional prison of victimhood it looks like they don't have room in their life to be concerned about other people's opinions. The attitudes of blame and hopelessness may have pushed them so far into their own personal jail that negative feelings are always present and so they never experience anything resembling a better life. Under those circumstances it is hard to worry about what they appear to be.

The last SPAR factor is Responsibility. Here we ask this question, "How do I feel about myself, due to my ability to meet specific standards?" This factor looks at how we feel as a result of comparing our actions against whatever subjective standards we apply to ourselves.

For the person carrying around the attitudes of blame and hopelessness this is not really a problem area that results in negative feelings. Having the ability to automatically blame others allows any sense of personal responsibility to fade out of life. In fact subjective standards would typically be made quite variable by a blamer so they can confirm that they are not responsible. An example of where personal responsibility fades out of life might be that they would travel across town to see a sporting event but not for a job interview. Or maybe a politician who gets significant support from a part of his or her electorate in one election and then loses it due to his or her immoral actions next time around. Being personally irresponsible is easy for a blamer.

When we look at the attitude of hopelessness we can see almost the same thing. The person who applies this attitude to situations where they can take some responsible action will often give up and do the easy thing, nothing. It is almost as if they just want to prove that they have no hope. Not taking personal responsibility for something allows a person to fail "because that is the way it is." In my earlier example about the situation in New Orleans, some people chose to not act in their own interests, to not be responsible, due to this attitude of hopelessness.

Blame and hopelessness do a lot to foster the behavioral trait of irresponsibility. This in turn reinforces the victim status and helps to keep those having these two attitudes in a form of slavery, the emotional prison of victimhood.

Some Final Thoughts

Victimhood is one of those prisons which can be escaped from with some reasonable effort, and under certain conditions. I noticed that some of the evacuees from New Orleans who came to Houston didn't go back. They found new jobs and new lives, they found hope. What was different about being in Houston as compared to New Orleans?

There were two big factors that helped them. First, there was the fact that they had physically relocated away from a center of influence. By this I mean that the cultural environment in New Orleans supported the attitudes of blame and hopelessness. This culture keeps people in bondage. Once some of them saw what it was like in another place, the door of the jail was opened. They were exposed to new attitudes from new people that challenged their old ones. They were exposed to new possibilities and hope for the future. Some of these displaced people chose to grab onto these new possibilities and hope and are now living a better life as a result of it.

The second factor was less government welfare. Please don't misunderstand me here. I'm a supporter of safety net welfare; we must as a moral society take care of those who aren't able to do it for themselves. The problem with welfare occurs when the state helps people stay in their victimhood prison. Once the evacuees were in Houston they could see how working was better than living off the state. Not only was the income better, the emotional benefit was enormous. With a meaningful job personal value or self-worth was more easily experienced. It allowed them to throw off the shackles of victimhood. All these people needed was a little help to get pointed in the right direction.

To me, what I observed during Katrina and the months that followed was very revealing. It clearly demonstrated that helping people in the wrong way can keep them in a form of servitude to the government. It seems to encourage some people to stay in the emotional prison of victimhood. As was shown by the whole hurricane episode, bad policy leads to a form of cultural serfdom in society. This serfdom contributes to some people falling into the emotional prison of victimhood. While I believe that there will always be some people who want to live that way, I also believe there are ways out and that our political leaders need to face these issues more honestly.

In Conclusion

The emotional prison of victimhood is filled with individuals who live a life of blaming others for their station in life, and who have an inclination of the Heart to hopelessness. There is a way out, and it involves making radical changes to the "stinking thinking" that comes from wrong attitudes, and changing the people you associate with who constantly drag you back into the jail.

18

PEOPLE PLEASING

Many professionals believe that every addiction has its roots in codependency.
Patrick McGinnis

This chapter, "People Pleasing", may be the chapter in this second book that most people identify with. People pleasing is the behavior in which individuals lose their own identity, make others seemingly more important than themselves and, as a result, live lives in which they are constantly trying to "do" for others as a way of getting their own emotional needs met.

Consider the case of Sammie. Sammie is an intelligent, attractive well-adjusted woman today, but it wasn't always that way. Sammie is a middle child; her older sister was a model child, and a little bit of a princess with her father doting on her. Sammie's younger brother was the "baby" and the family favorite; he could seemingly do no wrong. Sammie was aware that she was different, and she began to act differently from an early age. She wanted to be cherished like her sister and favored like her brother, but what could she do? Sammie had some gifts that she is now aware of. They were, and still are, the gifts of a keen intelligence and strong perseverance.

Armed with these gifts she set out to find the love she was desperate for from her parents, and in particular she wanted recognition from her father. She began to excel in her efforts at school, receiving kudos from her teachers, but not much more than well done from her mom and dad. The kudos and recognition from others really helped as they resulted in Sammie feeling valued. This was the general pattern throughout Sammie's early life, and then came the teen years. While her sister and brother were falling off the tracks into their own compulsive behaviors, Sammie chose a different path. Blessed with a keen sense of her own about right and wrong she stayed away from the common traps of sexual promiscuity and casual drug use. She opted for trying to be physically loveable, believing the messages the world sends that being thin equals beauty, and being beautiful means being loved. She became anorexic.

She left high school carrying this secret eating disorder still looking for her father's acceptance, which to her meant the valuing and acknowledgement of who she was. On the outside she was attractive, accomplished and self-assured, but on the inside she was still the little girl who wanted to curl up on her father's lap and be loved. Eventually she married a man who seemed like he was the one who would love her like she desired deep in her Soul. It was good, but only for a while, and then Sammie discovered that this man was deeply addicted to pornography. Without realizing it, Sammie took this as a challenge to prove to him that her love was better than the girls he was watching on the videos. She allowed the pornography to continue and worked hard at being the wife and excellent lover at home, hoping that he would stop needing the other women in those pictures. It was a battle she would quickly realize she could not win, and when she understood that he would not give up his pornography, the marriage broke up.

Still in her early twenties Sammie moved into several more relationships looking for recognition of who she was. After a few years wandering around in singleness she finally settled on a man who cared for her for who she was and who was significantly older than she. During this time she developed a career in a job where she had to serve other people's needs. This job allowed her to use her natural abilities and the skills she had developed over the years in doing things to please others. Although we might not recognize this job as a service job like cleaning buildings or being a waitress, that is exactly what it is, a high level service job. Sammie is a high-grade people pleaser.

Some readers will recognize the problem Sammie is challenged by; the world of psychology has given it a name - codependency.

Codependency as a separately defined affliction or disease or behavioral pattern (habit) whose subject has only really been identified as such since the early 1950s. Freud, Jung and their followers did some work on this topic in the late nineteenth century, but it wasn't called copendency, it was labeled as "unconscious forces", whatever that might mean. Real progress, however, in identifying what codependency actually is has only been accomplished since about 1970. The whole subject of codependency became popular psychology when the book "Codependent No More" was written and published by Melody Beattie in 1987. It is still a great read. One year before that in 1986, the first CoDA meeting was held in Phoenix, Arizona. CoDA is short for CoDependents

Anonymous, which is a 12-step program for codependency modeled after the AA and Al-Anon programs.

One of the difficulties this poses for us is the nascent nature of the subject. The psychological science work performed so far has failed to come up with a clean and clear definition of what codependency, or people-pleasing as I call it, actually is. In fact one of the best secular books on the subject of codependency, "Co-Dependence – Healing The Human Condition" by Charles L. Whitfield, a medical doctor, lists 23 separate definitions. To me, the best approach to trying to define what codependency is can be found in the material produced by CoDA, and is freely available on their website. They have a list called "Patterns and Characteristics of Codependence" which does the best job I've seen of helping understand what codependence is. I'm going to reproduce it here in its entirety. It is in four sections.

1.   Denial Patterns

- I have difficulty identifying what I am feeling.
- I minimize, alter or deny how I truly feel.
- I perceive myself as completely unselfish and dedicated to the well being of others.

2.   Low Self-Esteem Patterns

- I have difficulty making decisions.
- I judge everything I think, say or do harshly, as never "good enough."
- I am embarrassed to receive recognition and praise or gifts.
- I do not ask others to meet my needs or desires.
- I value others' approval of my thinking, feelings and behavior over my own.
- I do not perceive myself as a lovable or worthwhile person.

3.   Compliance Patterns

- I compromise my own values and integrity to avoid rejection or others' anger.
- I am very sensitive to how others are feeling and feel the same.
- I am extremely loyal, remaining in harmful situations too long.

- I value others' opinions and feelings more than my own and am afraid to express differing opinions and feelings of my own.
- I put aside my own interests and hobbies in order to do what others want.
- I accept sex when I want love.

4.   Control Patterns

- I believe most other people are incapable of taking care of themselves.
- I attempt to convince others of what they "should" think and how they "truly" feel.
- I become resentful when others will not let me help them.
- I freely offer others advice and directions without being asked.
- I lavish gifts and favors on those I care about.
- I use sex to gain approval and acceptance.
- I have to be "needed" in order to have a relationship with others.

In the book I mentioned earlier by Whitfield, the author says that some researchers estimate that 95% of adults in the US are codependent. If he is right, this means that most people reading this book ought to take an honest and close look at the list above as a step in improving their life.

Just to be honest myself, I compared my life with the list and I found that out of the total of 22 bullet points I can identify with 12 of them to some degree or another. This doesn't mean that I'm crazy or sick; it means I'm normal, in the sense of having some of the patterns, and I'm trying to be as honest as I can about it. Doing that little exercise means I'm moving out of denying that things aren't quite right and I'm moving into becoming healthier. Those who are unwilling or unable to do this may need the guidance of some trusted and safe friends to help them. If I can do it, so can you!

People-Pleasing Versus Pleasing People

You may have noticed that all of the "Pattern and Characteristics of Codependence" listed by CoDA are "I" statements. This observation gets at the underlying core basis or motivation for a person's people-pleasing habits. They are all about self, even though it may not appear that way to a casual observer. This means that codependency is a behavioral pattern a person exhibits which is born out of self-centeredness. It is fundamentally important to understand this and to differentiate it from pleasing people done with a motivation to help others.

As crude as it may sound, when we see people-pleasing in action, we simply have to ask the question, "What is the emotional payback?" The answer to that question will tell a person if he or she is observing someone who is exhibiting codependent behavior or someone who is not. I think it is important to get into the activity going on in the Soul of a person engaging in people-pleasing so we can identify motivations more easily.

Every person has an emotional state or condition at any one moment in time. They range from totally despairing to totally joyous, and there are many points in between. Some of these states persist inside a person's Soul briefly and some persist for days, months or even years. For the purposes of looking at our topic here I will be categorizing everybody in one of three groups.

- Generally negative.
- Generally neutral.
- Generally positive.

Most of us move in between these general categories as we conduct our regular daily life. We all would like to be able to remain generally positive all the time, and so much of our life's activities revolve around trying to get there. This is where people-pleasing comes in.

Throughout the series of these books we have discovered how negative emotional conditions are created inside a person, so let's assume we know that it happens. Then we have talked about how each of us desires to get rid of such conditions and how we often go about it. Some of us use drugs, some use sexual addictions and others religion. There is also a big group that uses people-pleasing in an effort to resolve the negative emotions which we sometimes carry around.

When someone has an internal generally negative emotional condition they are vulnerable to many things, one of these is that we can do something for another person and it results in us feeling better. Let me give us some examples to work with.

126

- A child who says, "Mommy, I love you" because he knows and desires a smile and an "I love you too" back.
- The wife of a drinker who fixes him a cocktail so that he will be "nice" to her in some way.
- The husband who, after a bad day, brings home a gift because he wants to have sex that night, which he knows will make him feel better.
- The volunteer at church who is miserable at home and is there early every Sunday, because he or she wants to be known as a helping person, and wants to feel wanted.
- The terrorist who kills himself for his or her god, because he or she wants to be rewarded.

It may be a stretch to put a child on a list with a terrorist for some, but it ought not be. The issue is identical; it is emotional payback. In each of the cases I've listed, a person is in a negative emotional state and is seeking to move into a better state by attempting to please another person. For a person who is simply trying to feel better, people-pleasing is a seemingly legitimate or acceptable way of doing it.

Now let's consider the person who is feeling emotionally okay, or as I've categorized them "generally neutral." This person may have a desire to feel better too. For much the same reason a casual drug user might take a pill to get a high, so might a people-pleaser engage in their habit of doing things for others out of self-motivation. Let's look at some examples of neutral emotional conditions in people and their people-pleasing activities.

- A child who cleans his room without being asked, because he knows it will please mom who will then give him the candy he likes.
- The wife of the alcoholic who buys her husband a fifth of bourbon because she likes giving gifts.
- The husband who has had a normal day and decides to take his wife out for a meal because he wants her to appreciate that she doesn't have to prepare something for him.
- The church volunteer who goes in a couple of times a week to be part of the prayer group, because she just feels better after she has done that.

- The terrorist who helps to train young men in the ways of terrorism because it feels good to manipulate young minds and be idolized by them.

Again the emotional objective of these emotionally neutral individuals is to feel better, just as it is for the generally negative group.

The emotionally positive group will also indulge in people-pleasing, but the motivation will be completely different. When we are in a positive emotional state we don't need to feel better, so jumping into self-indulgent people-pleasing has no payback. If we, when we are in a state of emotional positiveness, choose to people-please it is centered on their needs, not ours. Our emotional well-being is not determined by the other person being pleased.

When we acknowledge all I have just written about the emotional state of a person and their motivation for people-pleasing we can agree, in principle, with something stated earlier. The book by Whitfield suggests that 95% of all Americans are codependent to some extent or another. When we observe ourselves as a group, we can see that there are very few people who are always emotionally positive. This means that most of us are negative to neutral some of the time. When we see the 95% number, it actually makes sense.

Let's summarize this so far. People-pleasing to move from negative or neutral emotional states is motivated through self-centeredness and can be called codependency. People-pleasing while in a positive emotional state is typically other-centered and is healthy for both the pleaser and receiver. This doesn't mean that someone who is negative or neutral emotionally cannot be other centered, because they can, but it is rare and difficult.

The Four Horsemen of People-Pleasing

In the list developed by CoDA called "Patterns and Characteristics of Codependence" they identify four basic patterns. They are denial, low self-esteem, compliance and control; I call these the four horsemen of people-pleasing. I have to admit I named them after the four horsemen of the apocalypse (Found in the book of Revelation Chapter 6), because they mete out so much misery in the world. I want to look at how these four lead us into a life of trying to get our emotional needs met through pleasing others.

128

Denial Patterns

- I have difficulty identifying what I am feeling.
- I minimize, alter or deny how I truly feel.
- I perceive myself as completely unselfish and dedicated to the well being of others.

I think of the person struggling with this pattern as being lost. They seem to have no clue about what they feel most of the time. Sometimes they have some vague sense of what emotions are present in their Soul, but they can't label them. Shame is often confused with guilt, and anger with irritation. The denial causes confusion to the point that bad feelings are often shoved aside as trivial or are willfully relabeled, to enable one to sincerely deny them. I will hazard a guess that pain is the most significant emotion which is being denied through being minimized, shoved aside or relabeled. The individual dealing with this is truly clueless to the point that they don't know who they are, even though they may think they are okay.

When this problem of not knowing who you are becomes magnified in someone's life, they have much difficulty in knowing what they feel and think, they also have trouble being able to make decisions which make sense. To an observer they will seem somewhat irrational or even a little crazy. To be able to deal with all this confusion or craziness of the Soul, the lost person engages in significant people-pleasing. This enables them to be lost and distracted from having to deal with their emotional state in more healthy ways. It is as though they disassociate from negative feelings like pain or shame by distracting their Soul through doing things for others.

An example of this in action is the verbally abused wife. She has to be able to deny she is angry about what her husband is doing in order to survive. She will make excuses for his behavior in her own Soul, and also to friends who might see the abuse going on. She really believes she is helping her husband, or pleasing him, by being quiet and submissive. Long periods of being yelled at results in the poor woman acting like she is a beaten down dog.

Low Self-Esteem Patterns

- I have difficulty making decisions.

- I judge everything I think, say or do harshly, as never "good enough."
- I am embarrassed to receive recognition and praise or gifts.
- I do not ask others to meet my needs or desires.
- I value others' approval of my thinking, feelings and behavior over my own.
- I do not perceive myself as a lovable or worthwhile person.

The second horseman revolves around "not feeling good enough." This sense of not being good enough is typically planted in our Souls when we are young. It can happen directly when a parent says something that cuts you down such as, "You'll never amount to much." It can also happen within peer groups, particularly in adolescence. It seems to stop us in our tracks as we are developing the ability to handle our emotions, particularly our negative ones. In a sense this person, suffering from the second horseman, is also a lost person and can often be thought of as a lost child, and will often exhibit childish approaches to dealing with his or her situations.

The "unworthy" pattern can lead to a person doing things to the extreme. They can be one of the best workers you have if you are an employer because they can often go the extra two or three miles to get things done. As they try to feel better about themselves. They might also be the "life and Soul" of every party, cracking jokes, drinking to excess and generally trying to be loved, while feeling miserable inside. Or they can be the most religious person you have ever met, knowing the holy books inside and out, attending every Bible study and being at church whenever the doors open.

This person is a shell; they don't have any sense of who they are. They constantly try to "do for others" to get their need for significance met. They are lonely by choice because they don't feel worthy enough to have intimate friends. For them people-pleasing relieves the emotions that surround low self-esteem.

Compliance Patterns

- I compromise my own values and integrity to avoid rejection or others' anger.
- I am very sensitive to how others are feeling and feel the same.
- I am extremely loyal, remaining in harmful situations too long.

- I value others' opinions and feelings more than my own and am afraid to express differing opinions and feelings of my own.
- I put aside my own interests and hobbies in order to do what others want.
- I accept sex when I want love.

I think of a person dealing with compliance patterns, our third horseman, as a human chameleon. They tend to take on the role they think is expected of them. They can be uncannily accurate about what people around them are thinking and feeling, being able to instinctively read the verbal clues and body language we all give out. They can become so good at this that they can seem to be several different people wrapped up in one individual. This leads to their not having their own identity, but being all things to all people. Their "true self" becomes lost.

Being accepted is so important to the chameleon that they will go against the values, attitudes and beliefs of their own Heart; they will compromise. For example they may believe that sex outside of marriage is not appropriate, but get drawn into a sexual affair. The constant compromising makes them miserable, adding to their pile of negative emotions. This can lead to other compulsive behaviors, and eventually addiction, such as prescription pills or working out excessively.

In every relationship they have, the chameleon is seeking ways to please other people by taking on the other person's interests, even when they have no honest desire to do so. They want to please others, which is how they feel better. A married chameleon has a big problem. They work hard to please their spouse in their activity choices, even when they are not really interested. For example, a wife might go to a hockey game even though she finds the whole thing disgustingly violent. A husband might attend the ballet even though he is bored out of his mind. These kinds of compromises often lead to longer-term resentments and place unspoken, and sometimes unknown stress, on a marital relationship.

The human chameleon is very likely to be a major enabler. In order to meet their own emotional needs, they will actively support the people they care about in dysfunctional patterns of their own. A wife or husband of an alcoholic might be the person who keeps the liquor cabinet full. A parent will often give extra money to their teenage child even though they suspect they are taking drugs. A wife might live with her husband's use of pornography or a husband allows his wife to accumulate more shoes than she could possibly use.

The human chameleon is lost - they don't know who they are, or what they actually believe. They seem to be multi-talented and able to fit in anywhere. The truth is that; they are like the hamster on its wheel, running as hard as they can just to keep up.

4.   Control Patterns

- I believe most other people are incapable of taking care of themselves.
- I attempt to convince others of what they "should" think and how they "truly" feel.
- I become resentful when others will not let me help them.
- I freely offer others advice and directions without being asked.
- I lavish gifts and favors on those I care about.
- I use sex to gain approval and acceptance.
- I have to be "needed" in order to have a relationship with others.

The control pattern horseman breeds "control freaks." We all know people who are control freaks; but this type of control freak seeks to do their controlling or manipulation by pleasing others. The problem is that it is all from a self-centered motivation. In order to feel emotionally whole not only does this individual try to do what he or she thinks you want, they want to control the outcome too. Eventually this leads to them believing they know what is best for you and trying to control your thoughts, feelings and actions to get you to where they believe you should be. In the extreme, this person can become a monster to those around him or her.

As an example, we have all met fathers who have indoctrinated their sons into choosing the same college and career as their own. Right from the birth of their son these fathers are manipulating them in subtle and sometimes less than subtle ways. The control freak father forces the son to fit in with the father's expectations. As a people-pleaser, the father couches it in terms of assistance and guidance, trying to get the child to see and do things the father's way with hidden coercion. The poor boy may be another Beethoven, but his dad wants him to be a quarterback in the NFL. Very sad!

When the problem of being a control freak becomes severe, the individual loses touch with reality. They cross other people's boundaries whenever it suits them, trying to make it look like they are doing the other person a favor. The control freak people-pleaser seems to invade everybody he or she can and will often get upset and angry that his or her "help" is being rejected. This leads to others avoiding the people-pleaser, and the control freak is alienated from situations and relationships that he or she "needs" to live a fulfilling life. Yes, it is as sick as it sounds and this person needs serious help.

The control freak people-pleaser loses touch with behavioral norms, and with who they are. They are most likely to team up with another codependent as a marriage partner, a compliant codependent, and the marriage will have serious underlying issues. If one of the two of them ever tries to stop the madness and become healthy, a divorce is very likely.

The Loss of Identity

There is a theme which runs through all four of the horsemen. It is that the codependent doesn't really know who they are. We hear that term "who we are" frequently, but I'm not sure anybody ever defines it, so I'm going to do that for us now.

Who we are – Is the total of the distinguishing characteristics and personality we have.

I want to spend a moment on this to provide proper context for the chapter. The two components of who we are, in my opinion, are the characteristics and the personality. The characteristics of an individual are the nine things I outlined about the Soul in the first four chapters. They are a person's knowledge, understanding, wisdom, values, beliefs, attitudes, choice, control and gateway. Each individual has a unique set or combination of these nine characteristics. The personality of an individual is the way they combine these nine characteristics in their everyday life, in terms of their thoughts, emotions and actions.

There is a psychological concept used in some material written about codependency called "True Self." This, some experts believe, is the answer to the question we could all ask, "Who am I?" As best as I can figure it out, it is referring to the person you would be if you cleared all the clutter of codependency out of your life. I really don't like this idea as it does not deal with the truth and reality about a person and unnecessarily complicates the picture. To me the true self is what you are every day, including the clutter. The clutter is all the dysfunctions, the stinking thinking, the out of control emotions and the acting out which an individual engages in.

So when we talk about someone "losing themselves" or being a "lost child" what we really mean is that the person who they could be is hidden from view by the psychological clutter they carry. A lost identity is not exactly lost; it is hidden. When they work on removing the clutter, which is also called "being in recovery", they start to get a clearer picture of who they could be.

If you are reading this and realize that you connect with the thoughts I've written down about the four horsemen and lost identity, you are being prompted either by the Holy Spirit or by your own conscience to pay attention. Pay attention to what you may ask? The answer is this; there are some things cluttering up your life which it is time to deal with. It is up to you to act on it.

I have mentioned the Holy Spirit in the previous paragraph, and that leads me to asking what God says about the subject of people-pleasing.

A Scriptural Perspective

Did you know that the Bible could be thought of as the book of recovery? It is all about the fall of mankind and how his recovery is accomplished by Jesus Christ by His death on the cross and subsequent resurrection. Mankind "recovers" to the point that he is made whole again, if he chooses to accept Jesus as his personal savior. God wants us to "recover" - He gave us His son for this reason, and He still allows us the choice of whether to choose eternal life, which is total recovery, or eternal death, which is to stay in our dysfunctions. Which one do you want, life or death, recovery or misery?

The Bible is full of people exhibiting the dysfunctions of people-pleasing or codependency, and its consequences. I think one of my favorites is the story of Samson and Delilah. The whole story of Samson is told in Chapters 14, 15 and 16 of the book of Judges in the Old Testament, and it is an interesting read from the perspective of people-pleasing or codependency. I won't quote all the verses involved in the portion about him and Delilah, as it is a long tale; it can be found in chapter 16 of the book of Judges, in verses 4 to 21. I will summarize it in context here.

134

Samson met Delilah, and fell for her, and she became another of his female sexual conquests, but this one he was particularly eager to be with. She was tempted by the leaders of Samson's enemies, the Philistines, by a large sum of money to "give him up" to them by discovering the secret of his strength and passing it on. She seduced him and he played along to please her, but didn't tell her the truth. (This is common trait of a controlling codependent.) After many tries, she finally got him to give in and tell her the secret. Delilah passed it on to his enemies and he was made weak, then captured.

In this story we can see that both Samson and Delilah exhibited "control patterns' of people-pleasing. She used sex; he used his secret. She ended up betraying him, and he ended up a slave. I have put this in here to demonstrate a couple of things. First, that God will use or allow codependent people to achieve His purposes, and second, that the Bible doesn't shy away from how people really are. Now let's look at some of the things God addresses about being codependent more specifically.

Perhaps the most striking thing God says is this, it is found in the book of Galatians:

Gal 1:10 - For am I now seeking the favor of men, or of God? Or am I striving to please men? If I were still trying to please men, I would not be a bond-servant of Christ.

The author, the Apostle Paul, under the direction of the Holy Spirit draws a simple and very clear distinction between pleasing men and pleasing God. He draws this from his own life before he was a follower of Christ, a time when he actively persecuted Christians to the point of murdering them. This was done to please men, by his own admission. What God wants us to understand here is that if we indulge ourselves in people-pleasing, we serve men and not Him. It is a form of idol worship, although it is hard to see that, and even harder to admit if you are actually doing it.

Let's also notice that pleasing men (people-pleasing), is not actually condemned by God. This is because He sees the motivation as the issue, and therefore so should we. If we are motivated to serve or please people because God, through His Holy Spirit directs us to, then we are pleasing God not man, which is an appropriate action. If we have self-centered motivations such as social acceptance, personal financial gain or political power, then we are worshipping an idol.

I hope the stark contrast makes every reader think. In my opinion, self-centered people-pleasing makes a fulfilled spiritual life very difficult. Our desire to please others competes with our desire to please God; it gets in the way of our relationship with Christ. It is a barrier in two ways. First, it stops a person from becoming a follower of Christ - this is because they have made themselves their god. Second, it causes a competition within the Soul for intimacy. By this I mean that we will sometimes choose to seek intimacy with others and ourselves for spiritual fulfillment, instead of God. This is why Paul writes at the end of our verse, "If I were still trying to please men, I would not be a bond-servant of Christ."

How People-Pleasing Works

We have looked at how we live sometimes with lingering feelings inside our Soul; I have mostly called these unresolved emotions. We carry around feelings like shame, anger, defectiveness, inadequacy and worthlessness. These unresolved emotions are toxic to our Soul, because they are like a staph infection. They sit and remain where they are not wanted, and start to do damage. So often our response is to act out as a way of self-medicating by people-pleasing.

People-pleasing takes away the immediate effect of those lingering negative feelings by shifting our attention to the more positive ones we experience as we "help" others. Once the beneficial effects of the new positive feelings wear off, we are left facing the old negative ones again. This means that we have to do more people-pleasing, because it works for us, to self-medicate again, which results in more positive feelings, temporarily pushing away the negative feelings, which then come right back later. This is obviously a cycle.

To illustrate this, let's look at a simple and common situation; helping a co-worker. This is a true story, even if it seems a little strange. The guy who has the office next to me has an e-mail box that has more than 23,000 e-mails in it. He was complaining to me one day that his e-mail was very slow and it was interfering in his work. The problem was that he was looking for one particular e-mail from a few weeks ago. I slipped smoothly into my helpful co-worker mode and it felt good. He had given me an opportunity to people-please. I found the e-mail for him, but that wasn't enough - I wanted to fix his in-box. So I showed him how to permanently delete his unwanted stuff, and left feeling good, having done my good deed for the day. These good feelings were taken away instantly when I asked him the following morning if his e-mail was working faster. No, he said, because he had only deleted about two hundred of them. My people-pleasing self was very irritated.

Now, I could have fixed my irritation and his e-mail problem by more people-pleasing. But I immediately realized that it was a pointless exercise since my co-worker was really not interested in fixing the problem himself by learning what to do. This allowed me to not jump back into the cycle of people-pleasing followed by the return of the old negative feelings or even new negative feelings. My response to the problem the second time around was different. I asked him if he really wanted to take care of the in-box issue to the point he was willing to give up an hour or two to do the actual work of sifting and deleting. He said he wasn't right now. It still has not been done! He was being lazy, and probably being a people-pleaser by "letting me" do this for him. I was being a people-pleaser by taking on his task for the wrong reason. It wasn't about helping him; it was about me feeling good.

One other result of my mini story could have been me continuing to fix his e-mail problems. It would have enabled me to feel good for a while once every week or two. Ultimately though I would end up starting to resent it, and the good feelings would have gone away forever, and I would be left with an obligation to help.

Although my story is a simple illustration, I want to point this out. For people-pleasers, this kind of situation will occur frequently. They will have many opportunities to engage in their tendency to try to please others and this is where the real problem is found. The people-pleaser either has these "opportunities" to help others given to them or will seek them in their life's situations. Sometimes they will get a service job so they can be constantly helping others. If we multiply my e-mail story by a hundred or a thousand for a truly compulsive people-pleaser, we can imagine the outcome.

The outcome is this; we have an addict who is trapped in the emotional prison of codependency!

This addict looks just like a drug user. The drug addict gets his or her fix by taking something; the codependent gets it by people-pleasing. The drug addict is dependent on the drug; the codependent is dependent on people-pleasing. The drug addict is dealing with their negative feelings using additives; the codependent uses people-pleasing. The drug addict is acting out of self-centeredness; so is the codependent. The big difference is that drug addiction is generally socially unacceptable, and people-pleasing is generally socially acceptable.

So now you know. People-pleasing effects a person the same way chemicals do. This is why codependence may be the drug of choice of most people we know, and why it is an emotional prison.

SPAR and People-Pleasing

The elements of SPAR analysis are present throughout what I've already written, but let's go though it to consolidate our understanding of this very damaging compulsive behavior.

The first SPAR factor is personal Security. We ask this question, "How do I feel about myself?" We are looking at the issue of how secure we feel within our Soul. Personally I think this is obvious, our actions tell us something significant.

One of the ways to think about personal "Security" is by asking this question, "How safe do I feel, internally." The people-pleaser is saying through their actions that they don't feel safe just being who they are. This is why individuals we know who indulge in significant people-pleasing are often obviously insecure. Let's explore this thought a little more.

We have characterized acting out as taking actions as a response to what a person feels. When a person is feeling insecure or unsafe about themselves they want to get away from, to avoid, to suppress or to mask their negative feelings. It could also be put this way - they try to lose who they really are because they are insecure. One way to relieve themselves, or act out, is to conjure up new and better feelings by doing things for others, by people-pleasing. It is really very simple; replace one set of emotions with another better set and the insecurity seemingly goes away. The reality is quite different though.

The insecure person acts out by people-pleasing and has temporary relief from their own internal negative feelings. The word temporary is the key word here. All that is actually accomplished is a transitory substitution of one set of feelings with another. This is quite problematical because people-pleasing can be very effective at pulling off this substitution, and our insecure person can end up sub-consciously believing that the bad feelings causing insecurity are gone. They are not, and they always come back. They may not come back in a day or even a week, but they are hidden inside and will return.

This is the great poisonous effect of people-pleasing. It works for a while, we feel better, and we might even think we have been healed, but the basic problem of insecurity is still there. It is entirely possible to live a whole lifetime like this without really getting to the issue of our own insecurity. That is how strong a trap people-pleasing can be.

The next SPAR factor is "Performance." This helps us to understand how we feel about ourselves due to what we do. For a codependent this factor can turn into an unknown nightmare.

The performance oriented person who is people-pleasing is looking for basically one thing. They are expecting to have feelings of personal significance to spring up inside just because they have helped another person. These feelings of personal significance, like worthiness, capability and adequacy, then will push aside any negative feelings, and things will just seem better. This person will then carry around a sense of satisfaction, and be quite content, for a while. An example of this could be the individual who goes to volunteer at the Salvation Army soup kitchen at Thanksgiving. The codependent does it for self-centered reasons, for emotional uplift. The person not acting out will go out of love for other people and the meeting of their needs. The codependent will not be committed because their service depends on how they feel, and will tend to be unreliable. The second person, who isn't people-pleasing will tend to be a more reliable volunteer.

Just as in the case of the insecure person, the performance-oriented person will see the negative feelings they are trying to avoid spring back into life, and the cycle can start over again. The problem for this person is the unknown nightmares I mentioned a couple of paragraphs ago.

When we act out by people-pleasing, there can be two outcomes that might be troublesome to a codependent operating from a performance orientation. The first is that the people we try to please give us feedback which conflicts with our expected emotional objectives. They might reject our attempts to please them or accept the action but be ungrateful, which is another form of rejection. Since the performance oriented person is so tied to feeling better due to his or her doing things, this rejection is taken very personally. This rejection is then added on to the negative feelings that he or she is already carrying around. This kind of outcome is a nightmare because the performance-oriented person ends up being worse off than when they started.

The second nightmare is when failure occurs. When a performance oriented person people-pleaser fails to truly help another person, it can be devastating. Any negative feelings that were precipitating the people-pleasing get added to. So if he or she was struggling with the feeling of inadequacy, then they might now be dealing with feeling even more inadequate.

In both nightmare scenarios the same problem will come up. The people-pleaser will try harder to deal with their emotional difficulties by going deeper into their people-pleasing behaviors. This is much like going deeper into drug addiction. The performance-oriented people-pleaser can dig their personal emotional prison of codependence very deep indeed.

The third SPAR factor in that of "Acceptance." In my opinion this is the most easily spotted factor. It deals with the question, "How do I feel about myself, due to my perception of what others feel and think about me?" In other words, it is people-pleasing due to feeling accepted or unaccepted (rejected).

How many people do we all know who seem to take care of everybody else, but don't take of themselves or their immediate loved ones? I'm not talking here about the surgeon who seems to be called out all the time, or the pastor who is constantly working with his flock. I'm talking about the guy who stays late at the office to impress the boss, whose kids hardly ever see him. I'm talking about the mom who helps everybody on the street and neglects her home. I'm also talking about the husband who leaves his wife at home and goes out with his buddies a few times a week. And lastly, I'm talking about the wife who is constantly on the phone with her girlfriends, and shuts out her husband. These are all examples of acceptance driven people-pleasing, driven from a core of self-centeredness.

For some people the search for acceptance drives them to do things for others. We can actually learn this at a very young age. All of us with children have seen them do things for us to gain our acceptance, and we have all probably reinforced that behavior with rewards of some kind.

As an example, consider toilet training and how many of us have rewarded a child's success in this with words such as "What a good boy you are." When you think about this action/reward connection occurring many times for a child, is it any wonder that they might grow up relating doing things to being a good person and feeling accepted? Is it such a reach for us to now understand why some people emotionally link pleasing others to feeling okay about themselves and accepted?

This factor of acceptance, along with insecurity, are most likely the two biggest factors at work in codependents. Is it any surprise that a people-pleaser often looks like a totally emotionally needy person to those who are healthier? It is because they are! This behavior of people-pleasing to gain acceptance is almost a guaranteed ticket to the emotional prison of codependence.

The last SPAR factor is that of personal "Responsibility." How do I feel about myself, due to my ability to meet specific standards? That is what the question is here. I don't think this is as important as any of the other three factors, but it does have an interesting issue attached to it.

It is an issue of presentation. Sometimes you can ask a person why they are doing things, and they will tell you something like this, "Because I'm supposed to." Some religious people are like this. They think their god or their religion explains to them that they have to meet certain standards, and they choose to believe that. They then act in accordance with those beliefs. I call this the "presentation" of a reason why a person acts as a people-pleaser. However, when you take a closer look, the reality is different.

The presenter of people-pleasing through responsibility will also people-please when no specific standard is being applied. So a psychologist, or even a lay person, looking at someone who says they are "doing" to meet certain standards will have to look beyond this and get a more comprehensive picture of this person's activities. What they will almost always find is that an emotional issue like inadequacy or fear is actually the reason for the people-pleasing.

Now I'm going to take a final look at some other things that codependents might have going on.

People-Pleasing And Other Behaviors

I have seen enough people-pleasers to note one very common problem. They often indulge in other compulsive behaviors right along with their people-pleasing. I believe that codependency is a gateway problem that can lead to additional destructive behaviors. Let's look at some examples.

- A teenage girl will try to please her boyfriend by having sex; this can then lead to promiscuity.
- An adolescent boy tries to please his peer group by smoking pot; this might lead to expanded drug use.
- A man might go along with his boss to a "gentlemen's club"; this can lead to sexual escapades.
- A homemaker might go to daytime cheese and wine parties with some friends; she might then start sipping a little wine every day.

The point here is that we first see the more outward and obvious behavior, the drugs, drinking or sex, but the emotional basis for it began in codependency.

In my opinion, when we see a person struggling with a compulsive behavior or addiction, we will often find some level of people-pleasing behind it. This is why life doesn't always seem to get significantly better for the person who has overcome an addiction. The root cause never was related to the addiction, it was the codependency.

For an addict this can be very disheartening. He or she works so hard to escape one emotional prison, only to find themselves in another. Knowing this helps to understand why some people have what we label as an "addictive personality." This has implications for people who are choosing to be healed through recovery or treatment programs. The issue of codependency as a root of addictive problems needs to be seriously considered. Moving toward the full and complete knowledge of "who you are" would appear to be an important component of any treatment plan for an addict and particularly a codependent. Going from being lost, as a people-pleaser to knowing who you are, will go a long way toward breaking the chains that bind a person in an emotional prison.

In Summary

People-pleasing in an underestimated problem. The nature of codependency is such that it can look socially acceptable, and even socially desirable. The long term effects on a person are debilitating and can lead to significant other problems. These other problems might be addictions, and they also might be health issues like stress induced heart trouble or cancers. People-pleasing is truly an epidemic in this country, and is an emotional prison.

19

PERFECTIONISM

When you aim for perfection, you discover it's a moving target.
George Fisher

I would like you to meet Mike. Mike has the cleanest and most organized garage I have ever seen. When he had his house built, he had the builder leave the garage unfinished, because he wanted to finish it out his own way. Mike put up cabinets that went from ceiling down to about eye height; he put in a high workbench with a vice and other fittings. He had some roll in cabinets for his table power equipment and his tool chest was on wheels. He finished off the garage with white sheetrock, which was seamless. On this he hung all his yard equipment, with each piece having its own labeled spot. Everything was painted white, including the floor and ceiling; it sort of reminded me of one of those "clean rooms" that microchip manufacturers have. To cap it all off he didn't park his truck nor allow his wife to park her car in it. It was all very surreal.

How about Jacqueline? Her house was pristine. Every towel was folded in a special three way fold and hung up in matched pairs in every bathroom. The kids had been trained to fold them that way when they used those rooms and needed a towel. The bed was made as soon as she got up in the morning, and the kids knew better than to leave a crease showing on theirs. The kitchen counters were empty, except for the special built-ins that hid the microwave and coffee pot. The range had special covers that matched the wallpaper. The sink never had anything in it. Everything in this house matched everything else, the drapes, the wallpaper, the blinds, the carpet and the furniture were like something out of a magazine.

Mike and Jacqueline are perfectionists, and yes, they are real people I have met. They had some other amazing similarities too. Their families were both miserable. They were both quite obnoxious people to be around. People avoided them as much as they could, even the ladies Bible study group refused to go to Jackie's house. Perhaps you know people like Mike and Jacqueline, and you know why they had an awful relational life. We'll check in with Mike and Jacqueline later.

We have all met the Mikes and Jacquelines of this world. Indeed, some of us may even be like them. Did you know that the same kind of invisible forces which drive a person to drugs are at work here? The way these forces play out in the life of a perfectionist is different, but the origins of a drug or codependency addiction are the same as that found in a perfectionist. We are going to explore how this is true and how perfectionism develops. First though we must draw a line in between perfectionism and excellence, because they are different.

What is Perfectionism?

We need to clearly understand what perfectionism is and is not. So many perfectionists I've met hide behind the denial statement that goes something like this. "I'm just trying to do the very best I can." Or how about the religious version, "I'm working hard to do the best I can for the Lord, after all doesn't He call us to pursue excellence?" On the face of it there is nothing wrong with these statements, until we drill deeper. I want to explore these a little more.

A good place to start is with a definition of both perfectionism and the pursuit of excellence that are so often used interchangeably. These can be defined this way:

Perfectionism – a disposition to regard anything short of perfect as unacceptable.

The pursuit of excellence – a behavior where a sincere attempt is made to deliver the quality of excellence in an outcome.

There is a very important difference which these definitions highlight. Perfectionism involves a disposition, or an inclination of the Heart toward all things. It combines values, beliefs and attitudes and focuses them on all things, meaning both objects and people. If they fall short of what the perfectionist has as a standard, they are imperfect and get rejected. Pursuing excellence involves that same focus of values, beliefs and attitudes. However, it focuses only on the results of activities or behaviors and not on people.

Starting with this understanding let's look a little deeper into this difference to discover the core reason excellence and perfectionism should never be confused with each other. When values, beliefs and attitudes are applied within the Soul to a situation, emotions are born. I want to use the example of yard work to demonstrate a point here, mostly because I have a love/hate relationship with it and can see how easily perfectionism can creep in to this somewhat routine activity.

Start with the average yard - there are some beds with shrubs, bushes, and flowering plants, and there are lawns with a few trees. Now, let's get out there and start getting it into shape. First we start with the beds, and we have learned to begin by doing the clipping and pruning of the shrubs and bushes. The perfectionist will trim and cut until the bushes look exactly right, you know what I mean, "yard of the month" right. He or she will not experience the emotions of self-satisfaction and completeness until it is perfect. The person looking to do the trimming well has a different objective. Yes, they want it to look good, but the bushes don't have to be exactly rounded or trimmed down to match the bushes on the other side of the yard. The emotional end point for them is not self-satisfaction or completeness; it is job-satisfaction, the emotional feeling you get when you have completed a task to a reasonable standard and done it efficiently and effectively.

Let's keep working in our yard. This approach from the perfectionist, the one where each task has to be finished so that he or she feels self-satisfied and complete, is then used throughout the yard. The individual pursuing excellence also moves on seeking to do the rest of the yard well, and actually looks forward to finishing in a timely manner. He or she will then be able to experience the feelings that come from a job completed and done well.

Which of the two feels the best after the job is done, the perfectionist or the other? I would guess that both feel very good about the end product of all their work. However, which one completed the job in a timely manner? Which one is the most tired? Which one experienced the most anxiety as they worked? And, which one will still be worry-free after a week of growth of the yard?

What I'm pointing to here is the motivation behind perfectionism and comparing it to the motivation behind pursuing excellence. Another way of saying that is, what is driving the activity in each case? The driving force, stimulus or influence behind perfectionism is simply that if things

146

and people around the perfectionist are acceptable, then they, the perfectionists, feel acceptable. The perfectionist has at least a temporary sense that all is right with the world, and can experience some sensation of things being under control. For the individual working toward excellence it is different, they are satisfied with a job well done and it doesn't impact how they feel about themselves or the world around them.

As we allow that differentiation to seep into our thoughts, we can begin to see perfectionism in a clearer way. Perfectionism has its roots in how we feel about ourselves, which I'll be covering in more detail using the SPAR analysis later in the chapter. Perfectionism can therefore be thought of as an emotional state brought about through self-centeredness. Excellence is different and comes from the simple desire to complete a task well.

Since perfectionism can be thought of as an emotional state, we can see how if it becomes significant in someone's life, then it could lead to compulsiveness in doing things. This is when the perfectionist finds himself or herself in an emotional prison.

How Perfectionism Develops

Let's take a look at what is happening inside the Soul of a perfectionist. As is true of so many emotional prisons, the roots of this problem can usually be found in the early years of development. Consider as an example a home where a child overhears his or her parents arguing, a normal thing for a marital relationship. What if the child hears his or her name as part of this argument? They might assume that the quarrel is about them, even if it is not. One response of a child could easily be to flee due to his or her fear in some way, this could include physically or emotionally. At this point the child is not equipped to handle the overpowering grip that fear has on them, and they can't go to their parents with it.

Can we imagine what might be going on inside their young Soul? There must be something wrong, they are thinking, my parents are arguing about me. That means there is something wrong with me, I am wrong! In this state what can a child do? Some might hide in a closet until it is all over and seek reassurance about their family status later. Others might be able to understand on their own through watching and waiting that the fight wasn't actually about them. And some, destined to become

147

perfectionists, indulge in doing something which helps them to feel better about themselves. What might they do?

A younger child might rearrange their stuffed toys, or play-act a situation with those toys that has a good outcome. They might reenact the argument but change it so it is not about them, or they make it better. They might read or color in a book, or play with their dolls or toy soldiers. A slightly older child might seek his or her siblings, or go outside and do things with friends, or get on the phone. They might even attempt to be the peacemaker for the parents. It could be many things, all of which have one thing in common; in doing them the bad feelings they are having seem to go away.

Although I have used the example of the parental argument, I believe there are many scenarios that could initiate an emotional response inside a young person which results in them going to do things to feel better. The peak of getting a good feeling to replace the bad one a young person might be experiencing, is when they get feedback from another individual indicating that they are okay. When this happens it is likely that people-pleasing will be born inside the Soul.

It is all about feedback! As a person (young or old) gets feedback that supports and/or reinforces the actions of doing things as a method of dealing with their negative feelings, they will engage in that behavior more. If the feedback is only from the action itself or its results and has no other human involvement, it doesn't impact a person too much. If it is from a person, it is highly desirable. This is because a human source is verbalizing the confirmation that the individual is worthy, or adequate or acceptable. Once an individual begins to get this feedback they can get hooked on the "approval through feedback" mechanism. The most effective way to get it, of course, is to do things, and do these things well so that they receive recognition or praise from others.

Some of the Effects of Perfectionism

I tend to categorize the effects of perfectionism as either internal, which is having an effect within our Soul, or external, which is having an effect on others.

Internal effects tend to be about learned beliefs and acquired knowledge, the first influences the Heart and the second impacts the Mind. We'll start with the Heart characteristic of belief. Let's recall the way beliefs are developed in us as a starting point. In the early years beliefs are mostly formed through parental instruction. We learn our beliefs by absorbing information through the gateway of our Will. One of the learning mechanisms is through observing feedback. For example, we might ask our parents if it okay to hit our sibling with a stick. The feedback would be, "no, we believe that hitting your sibling with a stick is wrong."

When we are young, we might ask for feedback in some way, or we might be given it without asking. As we mature we still rely on feedback as a way of fine-tuning our beliefs, and we become more sophisticated about interpretation. We become skilled at figuring things out for ourselves, even if that means figuring things wrongly! For some of us this feedback either develops a new belief or builds on a belief which has already planted itself in our Heart. I want to stress here that these new beliefs are most often false beliefs in the sense of them being far from the truth. If the belief is that doing certain things well results in us feeling better about who we are, then we are on the way to becoming a perfectionist. This belief, or series of beliefs, works inside our Soul to produce actions that result in us doing things well. What is important to recognize is that a person "doing things well" for this reason of feeling better about themselves is motivated by self-centeredness.

The second major internal effect is that of impacting the Mind through the acquisition of knowledge. There is a point in the development of a perfectionist when the feedback about their task performance is very consistent in how much better it makes them feel about themselves. This is when a person knows that doing certain tasks will always result in feeling better. A kind of line crossing has occurred here. The belief, with its uncertainty attached, of "doing things well will result in me feeling better", is replaced by a more certain knowledge that "doing certain tasks well will always make me feel better." Let me give you an example.

Think about a young girl who first subconsciously notices that when she brushes her hair and tidies it up, either gets verbal rewards from others or feels better within herself. Over time, she unconsciously continues the pattern of fixing her hair when she is not feeling that well, emotionally speaking. The pattern gets established and she knows that she will always feel better about herself whenever her hair is fixed. I'm sure we all recognize that we know someone who is very particular about their hair, and not necessarily about other things. They can seem a little obsessive about their hair always having to be perfect, but they aren't. What they are doing is exhibiting perfectionism in action. Another point here is that if you ask them about it, they may admit they feel better if their hair is looking good, but they are unlikely to admit they are being a perfectionist. There are a lot of hair salons across America that depend on this very thing.

This last example of the perfectionism revolving around someone knowing and believing that when their hair is in good shape, they feel that they are okay, raises an important point. If you recall Mike and Jacqueline from earlier in the chapter, their perfectionism also revolved around a single activity or item. The important point is this; perfectionism doesn't have to mean that everything in a person's life is perfect. In fact my observation is that people with perfectionism in their life tend to have only a few things they are focused on that help them to feel better. As an illustration of this, and extending our hair example from the previous paragraph, reflect on the number of people who have their hair in great shape but never go to the gym. They are perfectionists about their hair, but not about their body condition.

Within the Soul of some of us, then, there is a tendency to learn that certain situations result in us feeling, at least temporarily, emotionally at peace with our life. It could be the completion of an activity to a high standard, like another of our examples from earlier; yard work. It could be how we look, visually or in our body shape. It could be keeping our desk at work completely cleaned off at all times. I'm sure the readers can come up with their own ideas on this.

The point here is to understand that just as in other emotional prisons, the feelings derived from the perfectionism are always temporary. Negative and nagging feelings such as unworthiness, inadequacy, and imperfection will resurface from wherever they were hiding. This results in the perfectionist having to keep on doing his or her thing to feel okay, and in some cases finding new ways to feel better. These new ways could be more perfectionistic behaviors, or they may start to become a new problem like drugs or overspending. Perfectionism is clearly an emotional prison.

There is a third major internal effect within the Soul of a perfectionist, and it combines the two other internal effects to develop something over time that lodges itself in the Heart. It is called pride. Pride can be defined as inordinate self-esteem. I like that definition as it carries with it the thought that prideful people carry around an elevated view of themselves. This is how it develops.

As the person begins to obtain new learned beliefs and knowledge, which we must remember are often far from the truth, some of them root themselves in very deep. They are reinforced, as our perfectionistic behavior is successful in relieving the negative feelings within our Soul. It is as if we form a covering of new positive feelings derived from our perfectionistic behaviors over the old, but still resident, negative feelings derived from emotional wounding, pain or other sources. In the physical world we call a growth over a wound on our body a scab, so I'm going to call this covering a "Soul scab." The problem here is that this Soul scab is covering unhealed or unresolved emotions.

When we do this, we have this situation. Underneath the Soul scab we have unresolved negative emotions. Collectively we can give a name to the effect they have on us, it is low self-esteem. The Soul scab is our Soul's response to the pain or wounds of low self-esteem, and it is comprised of more positive emotions. As we continue to be perfectionistic this Soul scab becomes hardened and entrenched in our Soul. We then act out of these combined positive emotions so as to deny what is underneath the Soul scab. The effect is to replace the covered over low self-esteem with a new higher esteem, which is called pride. Pride is therefore based on our response to difficult emotions, and is by its very nature a malfunction of our Soul.

Whenever we encounter a person acting out of pride or arrogance we can be sure that they are covering up or suppressing the truth of what is going on deep inside their Soul. A prideful person most likely has a core, but carefully hidden, belief that they are not a worthy person. Pride is an exceptionally strong dysfunction to root out of a person's Soul, and results in many obnoxious behaviors. Let me list a few; prideful people do these things:

- Know it all
- Put others down
- Are control freaks
- Keeps lists of offenses
- Think they are experts on everything

I'm sure you get the picture. Perfectionism can lead to many internal problems for the Soul; pride is probably the most damaging. These internal problems then lead to a rash of bad behaviors, which is our second major "effect of perfectionism." Let's look at that now.

The second category of "effects of perfectionism" is external effects. By this I'm referring to the effect perfectionists have on their personal environment, including their lifestyle and the people in their life. Perfectionists don't really appreciate this about themselves, but they can make life for those around them miserable. This is where the obvious needs to be stated - perfectionist are almost always control freaks. They seek to control everything and everyone around them as part of their perfectionism. This is sometimes the only way they can be sure that their negative emotional condition is dealt with. (For clarity, not all control freaks are driven by perfectionism.) Let's go though some examples; and maybe you'll be reminded of someone you know.

Mike is our clean garage guy from earlier in the chapter. If you recall, I mentioned that neither he nor his wife parked their vehicles in the garage, so it could be kept in perfect condition. This was a major problem for his wife. She was forced to have to go from her car to the house through their front door, and she had two major issues with this. First, when it rained, she got wet, and it was made worse when she had the kids or friends over or had been shopping. Second, her personal security was threatened. When there were a rash of car-jackings and home invasions reported, it was done through criminals following ladies home. Mike's wife was too afraid to use the garage. She was more afraid of Mike than of being kidnapped! Nothing ever actually happened, but this does provide us with an example of how miserable a wife can be with a perfectionistic husband.

And now we come back to Jacqueline. Her husband and kids had to keep everything immaculate, everything revolved around keeping mom happy. The old idiom, "Ain't nobody happy, if Momma ain't happy" was unfortunately true in this household. Even her friends were affected - they simply avoided going to her home, even though Jacqueline really wanted to host a Bible study there. Her study friends from church found themselves lying by making excuses to not do the study at her house. Jacqueline was grieved, after all she had the "perfect" home for hosting, and she took it personally. Not one of her friends had the courage to explain what the problem was.

Have you ever had a boss who wanted everything to be done perfectly? I used to be like that. I wanted all my employees to do things well, and do

152

it now and do it my way. I certainly got things done, but I'm equally certain that I made life difficult for people who reported to me. My perfectionism blinded me to other people's hidden talents and abilities, It made it difficult for them to come to me with their ideas and I was basically a benevolent dictator and a control freak!

I think that you probably get the idea by now. Perfectionism is like a monster from a Greek myth. It affects the individual who is afflicted with it, and it has an effect on everybody who is close. It is often difficult to spot and it is difficult to deal with if you are not the one who is carrying it. Individuals cursed with this problem often have a hard time seeing it in themselves. They are truly trapped in an emotional prison.

Variations of Perfectionism

There are some other ways perfectionism is expressed in our lives, so I thought I would spend a moment or two on these. I'm going to briefly look at two of them; the "procrastinator" and the "mess up."

The procrastinator is a perfectionist who waits to complete his or her planned activity until they think or believe they are ready to do it. Unfortunately they wait so long for conditions to be perfect that they get squeezed on their time to finish a task. This results in a tremendous or intense time of activity and sometimes results in a sub-par job being done, but most often it works out to the perfectionist's satisfaction. The perfectionist gets the good feelings he or she is looking for, but there are a couple of costs. The first is that they have a belief that they can wait until the last minute to do something; eventually this will backfire. A backfire could result in a lost job, or personal financial losses, or a failed college exam and most certainly will result in a negative emotional event. The second cost is stress, which in this case would best be thought of as emotional pressure. Over time stress finds its way into our physical health, with resultant immune system failures such as a propensity to get sick, and in the extreme, things like cancer or heart problems can arise.

The "mess-up" is a perfectionist who really struggles with failure. This is a counter-intuitive person. They mess-up and fail in an obvious way because they want to create a big space between the standard they are applying to a task and the actual job they do. It creates a picture that the task was impossible to complete in the time available and to the standard applied. These are the people that seem to sabotage their own lives.

Does the Bible have anything to say about Perfectionism?

My question above has an obvious answer, yes. That is because the Bible has something to say about most dysfunctional behaviors which you will run across. I have yet to be presented with a dysfunction that is not covered in Scripture, and perfectionism is fully covered, in my opinion, by this verse. It is from the book of Colossians:

Col 3:23 - Whatever you do, do your work heartily, as for the Lord rather than for men.

Let's look closely at what our verse is saying. Whatever you do, do it heartily, as if you were working for God, and not for people. The Greek translated to "heartily" here is actually two words that literally mean "out of the Soul." In this Scripture God has linked working well to believing in Him, and His guidance for the conduct of our lives.

Follow me on this. Since all our behaviors originate in our Soul, we combine our Mind, Heart and Will to accomplish every task. If we are working out of unbelief, we will be disobedient to God in the area of perfectionism. In our Heart we carry our values, beliefs and attitudes. If we don't value God, don't believe His words and have the attitude that "what I say is more important than what God says", we are living in the sinful states of unbelief and pride. When we engage in perfectionism we are working for our own emotional benefit, and not for God. No matter how we try to sugar coat it, we are being disobedient to God's instruction. The sin of disobedience, exemplified by doing things your own way as we do in perfectionism, is rooted in unbelief.

This is a tough thing for us to grasp. We can all understand the linkage I have discussed, and might even agree with it. The problem with accepting that perfectionism has a root in unbelief in God and His authority, is the previously mentioned confusion between excellence and perfectionism. God supports excellence in His word, He does not support perfectionism. Perfectionism is an emotional prison, which is why God warns us about it.

Perfectionism Looked at through SPAR Analysis

As we have done throughout the second part of this book we'll take a look at the four SPAR factors that help us understand a little more how and why people get into their dysfunctions, which in this chapter is perfectionism.

The first factor is personal "Security", where we look at the question, "How do I feel about myself?" As we have alluded to earlier in the chapter, the answer to this question may be central to the development of a perfectionist. In our lives we find ourselves in situations where negative emotions about ourselves are created inside of us. If we discover that doing things well helps us to replace those feelings, even temporarily, we are on the road to developing perfectionism.

As we live our lives we may continue to resort to engaging in perfectionistic behavior whenever we feel negative about ourselves. At some point it crosses over from being a behavioral response to some negatively charged emotional situation into a habit or even a preventative activity. Perfectionistic behavior might become the daily norm for an insecure person, much like some people take an "upper" style drug each day to feel better in their Soul.

Our second SPAR factor is "Performance." Here we are asking "How do I feel about myself, due to what I do?" This might surprise you. While it is true that a perfectionist has to do things well to accomplish his or her goal of feeling better, it is not always about everything he or she does.

Someone driven by personal performance is concerned with what they do, not what they do well. This means that although a performance driven person might be prone to perfectionism, it is not always the case. The performance driven person is motivated in their performance mostly by the fear of failure. The perfectionist is motivated by the need to remove their negative emotions, and if you wanted to give this a fear name, it is a fear of what they are feeling. This is why I don't think this factor has a lot of influence over a perfectionist.

Our third factor of "Acceptance", is highly significant. Here our concern would be, "How do I feel about myself, due to my perception of how others think and feel about me?" When you initially ponder this question there is a tendency to come to a conclusion of this type, "It looks like perfectionists don't really care what others think." This is because they go right ahead and indulge in their perfectionistic activities despite others expressed opinions or comments. But the reality deep within them is that they do care what others think of them.

If you recall earlier in the chapter I mentioned that the most important type of feedback for a perfectionist comes from people and not the outcome of an activity or doing a job well. This is because personal acceptance validates that they are okay. Maybe the best confirmation of this is to think of a prideful person, how do they respond if they are not accepted? When you prick their bubble, it is as if you have ruined their life. Some of the responses are anger, depression, withdrawal into loneliness, and shame. These are all powerful emotional reactions, and they all come out of not being accepted.

Our last SPAR factor is "Responsibility." The question here is, "How do I feel about myself, due to my ability to meet specific standards?" If the perfectionist struggles with this question we ought to feel sorry for him or her.

A person who grapples with perfectionism will often have a lingering doubt about the end-point of their behavior. Going back to the yard clean up, an example might be whether the bushes are trimmed down to the right height? Can you imagine how it might drive a perfectionist a little crazy to have a doubt about that? Whenever a perfectionist senses that maybe things aren't quite as perfect as they should be, he or she gets a little bent out of shape. They start to feel a little less positive about themselves, their personal pride is challenged and their Soul scab gets a tear in it.

However, when a person is somewhat driven by meeting specific standards in the pursuit of feeling better, perfectionism is a normal response. Since we have already covered this connection earlier I won't say much here. What I do want to do is point out that this factor tends to push the perfectionist to ever increasing levels of achievement, or dysfunction. Also, when the perfectionist, driven by standard chasing, eventually reaches their limitations, they are vulnerable to beginning other types of compulsive behaviors. For example a perfectionist may begin having a cocktail or two to help with the pressure of being perfect.

Summarizing the Situation

Any person alive today could be a perfectionist. It doesn't matter what a person's background is, perfectionism knows no cultural or social boundaries. A person living in a mud hut or a mansion could be a perfectionist. It is all about whether they deal with their collective negative emotions by using perfectionistic behaviors to cover them up or not. Perfectionism can become such a way of life that a person is pushed by their emotions every day toward the deep hole of an emotional prison.

20

RISK

Gambling: The sure way of getting nothing from something.
Wilson Mizner

Risk could be the strangest sounding emotional prison that there is. When I was laying out some of the subjects I wanted to cover, I knew I wanted to address gambling. Then as I got thinking, which is always dangerous for me, I came to understand and acknowledge that there is much more to this risk issue than gambling.

Let's start by agreeing on what risk actually is. The term risk tends to be used in two different ways, as a noun and as a verb. We will be using the word risk both ways in this chapter, and we'll also use some substitute words, so let's lay these things out here.

- Risk as a noun, it is the possibility of loss or injury.
- Risk as a verb, it is to expose to hazard or danger.
- Risk substitutes include danger, jeopardy, threat, peril, hazard, menace, chance, gamble and venture.

Do you connect with any of these words? I certainly do and as I reflect back on my life, I can see that there were so many times that I took risks. Let me run through a list, which will provide some examples of riskiness.

- Climbing trees; big trees
- Swinging from tree to tree, like the character Tarzan
- Stealing the neighbor's fruits and nuts, from his trees
- Setting fire to trash cans
- Driving fast, very fast
- Rock climbing
- Leaving my country of origin to work overseas
- Scuba diving, sometimes with sharks
- Coming to the US with next to nothing
- Becoming a Christian

For the record, the scariest physical thing on the list is rock climbing, the scariest psychological action was coming to Christ.

I imagine some people might want to know about that last comment. The actual day I finally gave in to God's knocking on my Heart and let Jesus in was a risk day. I had been going to church for quite a while and had learned much about Christ. The preacher had given me a book written for people like me, the intellectual who always questions everything. It was called "Mere Christianity", and was written by C. S. Lewis. On that day, the associate pastor gave an altar call, which they didn't always do at this church. He said something that just clicked in my mind. He said, "Coming to Christ is always a risk, because you don't know for sure what is on the other side of your decision." I suddenly realized that this was the missing piece, it was the truth. From my perspective, I could never know with a 100% certainty what was on the other side of this decision, no matter what anybody said or wrote. I had to take the risk. Of course I know now that that moment was a step of faith, and it took someone putting it in words I could relate with to open my eyes to what I needed to do.

Although I have a history of risk taking I wouldn't regard myself as a major risk taker. There are people we all know that like to do extreme sports or bungee jumping or free fall parachuting whenever they can. There are others that like to experiment with new illegal drugs or other strange chemicals. And there are still more who like to constantly encounter new and fascinating people. Some like to throw dice or play cards and put their financial future on the line. Risk-takers of this kind choose to create some form of danger in their life, and it is a pattern of behavior. It is these kinds of risk-takers we will be talking about in this chapter.

There are others who look like they are taking a risk, but it is done with caution and a whole different objective. An example might be a child who climbs on a chair to reach something high or a person driving a new route from one place to another. These are task-oriented risk-takers, not emotion-oriented. Once they have accomplished the task after taking a risk they are satisfied and don't have a need to take another risk. An emotion-oriented risk-taker will only feel temporarily satisfied with the outcome of their risky activity, and will choose to do it, or other risky activities, again.

Why Do People Take Personal Risks?

This is a very good question, "Why do people imperil themselves?" We can even see this in young children - some are daring and some not. The answer to this is both simple and complex. The simple, but uninformative, answer is this; it is for a personal emotional objective. To get at the truth of this we need to break down what these personal emotional objectives might be, and identify categories of risk takers by their objectives. Before we look at the breakdown of objectives we must acknowledge some things about risk-taking. I call these the four potentials:

1. The potential for failure
2. The potential for blame
3. The potential for losses
4. The potential for reward

All four of these are obvious to most of us, but it is by taking a deeper look at these four that we can derive the emotional objectives of a risk-taker.

The Potential for Failure

When someone knowingly takes a risk they understand that there is a possibility they will fail at whatever they are doing. The degree of risk, or put another way, the amount of danger involved, seems to be less important than the actual taking of it. The doing of the risky activity is important, not what the outcome, failure or success, might be. We need to look into the Soul of this kind of risk-taker.

Some individuals live life with values, beliefs and attitudes in their Heart that can be summed in this simple statement, "I am what I am." They may be living life with a sense of hopelessness, accepting that they are what they are, and it won't get better. They are somewhat comfortable with their perceived status of what they are, and live with a sense of contentment. They may also believe they are what they are, but carry around a sense that things ought to be better, and are a little frustrated. This seeming categorization is actually better thought of as a spectrum where individuals are anywhere on it from the hopeless sense at one end to the frustrated sense at the other.

The key to understanding what is going on inside this person is to focus on the statement, "I am what I am." This is a summary statement that identifies who a person is by what they are; it links their personhood to what they generally do. This means that the emotions that are routinely generated in their Soul about themselves revolve around their activities, as they equate who they are with what they do. An individual like this will have a hard time identifying the truth that they are a unique person at all times no matter what life brings.

For some of the "I am what I am" people, the potential for failure represents emotional opportunity, and the taking of a risk is entirely logical. For these people failure means that they confirm their own thinking and feeling about themselves. The statement "I am what I am" is validated. Validation is always an emotional positive; even inappropriate or incorrect validations feel positive to the people receiving them. In this case we are talking about a person self-validating, which means that he or she is both taking the risk and upon failure, receiving an emotional benefit.

If the "I am what I am" person succeeds in something after taking a risk, even if they are not playing a slot machine, they still hit a jackpot. Emotionally speaking, success from taking a risk for this group means that they get an emotional lift. The "I am what I am" becomes "I am better than what I was", and at least for a while it feels good. This is similar to what a drug addict might feel when they get a high. It is always temporary. The "I am better than what I was" bubble gets burst because nothing has actually changed inside the Soul, the values, attitudes and beliefs have not altered at all, and the old "I am what I am" will come back. I'm sure that you can immediately see we have the beginnings of an emotional trap developing here. A gambling addict would be a typical "I am what I am" risk taker.

The "potential for failure" type of risk-taker therefore may have either or both of the two emotional targets discussed above. They are:

- Validation of personhood
- Emotional boosting

These are our first two emotional objectives, or answers to the question, "Why do people take personal risks?"

161

The Potential for Blame

Some of us are basically irresponsible in our behavior. Some are highly irresponsible, and others less so. To be able to stay in our irresponsibility we have to be able to blame other people, the system, or in the case of religious folk, an unseen spiritual foe.

An irresponsible risk-taker is an individual that is more self-centered than most. For them the world revolves around them and their needs and wants, even to the point that they believe the world owes them. This is the kind of person that won't get a job because he or she thinks that their family, the government or maybe even God will come through and provide whatever they need to live. That is a presumptive risk, presuming on the benevolence of others. Why would anybody adopt this kind of behavior? One of the reasons is that this irresponsible person will be able to, at least in their own Mind, be able to blame others if they don't get fed or clothed or housed.

Another irresponsible who blames is the person who undertakes a risky action of some kind and consciously or sub-consciously knows that they will blame another person if things go wrong. A good example of this is Adam back in the Garden of Eden. He blamed Eve for his action of eating the forbidden fruit, and then also blamed God because He (God) had given Eve to him (Adam). Have you ever heard someone say, "If this goes wrong I can blame so-and-so?" That is risk-taking with the potential for blame.

What is going on in the Soul of such a person? Simply this - being able to blame seems to help avoid negative feelings. Did you notice that I said, "seems to?" That is because there is an illusory effect occurring here, an illusion within the Soul. We have run across a phenomenon before where we humans are consistently confusing who we are with what we do. We have another example here with the irresponsibles.

Let's assume that a person has taken a risk, which can be doing something or doing nothing, and failed at it, and that they are an irresponsible who is blaming another person. Inside the Soul of this person a set of feelings will arise as a response to the outcome of the hazardous action taken. Certainly this person will be aware that they have failed, and be able to think, "I have failed." Usually what happens though, is more likely to be an emotional response such as, "I feel like I am a failure." Do you see the subtle, but powerful, difference? Instead of thinking that a failure has happened and then moving on, the person relates the failure to who they are. Instead of "I failed" it is "I am a failure."

The irresponsible takes this one step further. They may feel like a failure, but they then assign blame to another. This allows them to create what I call an illusion. The illusion is that they are not a failure, because they had no control over what happened anyway, it was someone else's fault; therefore they are not a failure. This is, of course, a big lie. The failure is their fault, and they have failed as a result of their own choices and actions.

The illusion enables the irresponsible to deny or hide his or her real feelings by lying to themselves that someone else is actually responsible. Earlier I said that the illusion seems to help avoid the negative feelings that come with failure. This is because those feelings don't go away; they stay right there where they are created, in the Soul. To keep them suppressed, a person has to continue to lie about who is responsible. For some people to let these emotions come out may overwhelm them, and that is why they stay in the illusion, and stay in a blaming mentality.

The potential outcome or result for a blame type of risk-taker has their own emotional objective:

- Avoidance of negative feelings.

This is the third emotional objective or answer to the question, "Why do people take personal risks?"

The Potential for Losses

As crazy as it may sound some people take risks when they know they can lose something significant. Most often it would be something material, typically money, but there are other losses that can also be important to us. The most obvious is the potential for loss of one's physical life. Other losses could be the loss of one's health or livelihood. Another truly significant potential loss is the loss of relationships.

Going back to my personal risk list at the beginning of the chapter I'm sure you can spot several items like this. The rock climbing, the scuba diving, and the fast driving are all examples of risk with the potential for loss of life. So, why did I do such things? Why do others skydive or bungee jump or race motorcycles or drag race? And why do some people make all or nothing bets in the casinos, or act obnoxiously at work to the boss? Finally, why do some people have a string of illegitimate relationships risking the loss of family?

It is a big "why" question. Looking inside the Soul of others and myself we can catch flavor of "why." Starting with the reasonable premise that there are unresolved negative feelings lingering inside a Soul, we can see that doing something radical to uplift oneself is very attractive. Putting up a bet, such as your own life, means you would have to survive the odds of losing something significant through your own actions to be a winner. What does a person win? They win a euphoric moment, an emotional high. It could last just a short time as in winning a bet on a horse race, or longer as in an extra-marital affair. It is still the thrill of the moment, but more than this, it is the creation of positive emotions that are the goals. As in all the attempts to dull, avoid or deny any innermost negative feelings we have, it succeeds for a short while, and then the old feelings reappear.

Therefore the potential for loss type of risk-taker has a simple emotional objective.

- Creating positive emotions

This is our fourth emotional objective.

4. The Potential for Reward.

This is the only one of the four potentials that has some element of healthiness in it. We have all heard the terms risk and reward put together in the context of normal life. It is part of the process of growth both in our material world and in our psychological world. It is the only aspect of risk that is condoned by Scripture. There is a parable called the parable of the talents, taught by Jesus, found in the Gospel of Matthew, Chapter 25, verses 14 to 28. It talks about using what you have been given through normal activity and gaining more, which is what we call growth. It is the risk-taking I undertook when I chose to accept Christ as my savior. When a person undertakes anything based on faith then he or she is risk-taking with the potential for reward.

However, there are two unhealthy aspects to risk-taking with the potential for reward. The first is where a person takes too much risk for a small or even no reward. The second is where someone takes a risk for too large a reward. Let's unpack these two.

Would you run into a busy street to pick up a penny? I hope not! This is a simple example of undue risk for a small reward. Some of us are penny-pickers in other ways. How about the college kid who drinks enormous amounts of alcohol to gain the temporary acceptance of his new buddies? Maybe you relate to this next example - telling a lie by embellishing the truth of a story to your co-workers in order to impress them. My last example may surprise some people at first, as it seems counter to what we call the American Dream. I have seen so many people who work very hard, some successfully and some not, to acquire position or more income, but lose other things like health or family. Jesus spoke to this when he said the following:

Mt 16:26 - For what will it profit a man if he gains the whole world and forfeits his Soul?

In the context of big risk/small reward, Jesus is asking the question, Will you give up your Soul for all the rewards the world offers? While Jesus was referring to the ultimate choice we all have to make, whether to follow God or not, this verse has other applications here.

When we chase the things of this world, things like money, fame, power or the approval of others, we take a risk of giving up our integrity. Integrity here means the healthiness of our Soul. Don't we see this happen all around us? Think of all the Hollywood stars that have to compromise themselves, lose some of their personal integrity, to get ahead. Staying in Hollywood we can see how important it is to remain famous to these people, so important that they will say and do things that are just bizarre. Look at all the people who were going to leave the US if George Bush got elected. Did any of them do it? No, but they all lost some of their personal integrity when they didn't follow through on their promises. They damaged a piece of their Soul.

What is causing people to take big risks for small rewards? Economists and business analysts have a method for looking at risk and reward that would seem to apply here. It is called cost-benefit analysis. Most of us have heard of this, but may not have used it. It is basically a simple look at the question, "If I spend a certain amount of money on a certain project, what will my return be, in financial terms?" Using this philosophical approach we can get at why a person would take a big risk for little reward.

When an analyst looks at a business project, part of what he or she investigates is when the expected financial return will occur. If the financial return is not expected to occur for 20 years, the project is likely to be rejected. If the return is expected next year, the project is much more viable and rewarding. That is how it is for our big risk taker who is looking for a small reward. They are looking for an immediate return on, or reward for, their risk-taking. The business analyst, however, looks at his or her analysis with a dispassionate eye, meaning with a low emotional input. The risk-taker in this case is not that rational and engages in emotionally charged decision making, usually resulting in bad choices.

Some people, when faced with choices will choose to act to immediately emotionally gratify themselves, and that is what the big risk/small reward individual is doing. Their instantaneous personal analysis of a situation provides the impulse to act irrationally, and often to the point that they ignore the potential downside of their choices. Let's look at one of the examples we raised already.

The Hollywood stars who were all going to leave the US if George Bush got elected were acting on impulse. They expected the reward of adulation from some of their peer group or adoring fans. They would probably say that they were making a sincere political statement, but their actions say otherwise. George Bush did get elected, and they stayed. Their so-called political statements were nothing more than childish impulses. These statements were made for the specific purpose of feeling better about themselves. The two rewards here were perceived (by them) higher acceptance from others and immediate personal emotional self-gratification.

Another example of big risk-taking for small reward is where a small child is lured by an adult pedophile. The adult knows that some children will go for the ice cream or candy which is the small reward, and take a big risk for it, like getting into a stranger's car. The child in this case is not properly equipped to assess risk and reward and will make the choice for immediate self-gratification. In this the Hollywood stars and the child have acted in a similar fashion.

Our first "potential for reward" risk-taker therefore has the personal emotional objective of:

- Immediate emotional self-gratification

This is our fifth emotional objective.

The second potential for reward risk-taker is the one who takes risks for big rewards. Properly done this can actually be a reasonable way of conducting parts of life, and is entirely rational and growth producing. The single best example I can give of this is where we invest our discretionary monies. If we invest rationally and prudently we would diversify, lowering our overall risk, and seek reasonable gains. Some of us however like to play the market and invest in oil futures or corn options. These are the types of risk for big reward-takers I'm going to talk about, these are the gamblers.

My perception of gambling and gamblers is that they seem to have one of three different objectives. I'm going to label them, "rescue-seeking", "thrill-seeking" and "tentative."

Rescue seekers are the kind of people who take a risk to gain a reward that they think will secure their future. This is the person who might have left his or her family and seek their fortune in the gold mining business back during the California gold rush. Some of those who took the legendary wagon trains west in the early part of US history were rescue-seekers. More modern day versions might include the independent wildcatter looking for that elusive black gold, or the person looking for buried or sunken treasure. It is all about, "When I strike it rich, I'll be able to, (fill in your own blank here)!"

To some it might appear that a person gambling for a big reward is motivated by greed, but I don't believe this is so. Once a person has achieved a comfortable level of security, whatever that might be, that is when greed might manifest itself. Greed involves an entirely different set of psychological deficiencies, and can be an emotional prison of its own. I think the original motivation for this type of gambler is that they want to be in control of their own life, and be "rescued" from being controlled by other people or circumstances.

Isn't it interesting that some people will risk everything they have, taking actions that risk the very things that are most precious to them, to gain security? I believe that at some level we all connect to the idea that, "If I just had money, acceptance, fame, power or something of one's own choice, everything would be okay." It is as if we, all humans, have been built with a hole inside us that needs to be filled. It means that we are all searching for the thing that will fill it. The gambler is willing to go to great lengths to fill his or her hole by attempting a self-rescue.

Looking at what is going on inside the Soul of a rescue seeker, we can notice some things. They are not driven by bad feelings that linger, like so many others who are trapped in emotional prisons. They may have the negative feelings we have seen throughout the book, but are not being pushed by them. The pursuit of big rewards is to fill a void inside, and when this void is filled, they will have control over their own life, including negative feelings. To me, looking at this kind of risk-taker, I see more of an emotional pull toward getting trapped in an emotional prison, than a push, which is more common.

The personal emotional objective here is:

- The filling of an emotional void by achieving control over their life

Our sixth emotional objective!

Next we come to the thrill seeker. This is the person who is risking to get high rewards, not for the reward itself, but for the emotional rush that comes with the gamble. We are all familiar with them; some of us even like to indulge in this ourselves. This is the gambler who is not gambling to win the money, but to get the emotional high.

Inside the Soul of the thrill-seeker those negative feelings that we discuss so often, are lingering. The thrill-seeker is acting just like a person using an upper in that they are seeking to quickly improve their emotional state. Their fix is not the result of a drug acting on them; it is the result of participating in the gambling activity. Just as with a drug, once the time of action is over, an immediate emotional drop-off occurs. The thrill-seeker then begins to seek his or her thrills again. As this activity becomes more pronounced it will take over a person's life, just as drugs will.

One interesting aspect of thrill-seeking is our cultural celebration of it as an acceptable part of life. As I was writing about this type of individual I got to thinking about how many movies have been made, and stories written that detail the seeking of the thrill. It is a form of glorification of this damaging activity. The recent "Oceans" movies are a good example. They are very entertaining movies that show the planning and execution of sophisticated casino robberies. Most of the time in the movies is about the pursuit of the goal, the prize, the money. When the bad guys finally achieve the success of the executed plan, it is almost a let-down. Watching this kind of movie allows us all to be vicarious thrill-seekers!

The emotional objective of the thrill-seeker is:

- An emotional high

This is our seventh emotional objective.

The last risk-taker is the "tentative." I have given them this label because they want the big rewards, but are unwilling to use a large amount of their resources to achieve the big win. There is nothing wrong about being tentative in itself - it indicates some level of prudence, but there is an aspect of it that is of concern.

When prudent men or women takes a small risk for an expected favorable return, they have a reasonable grasp of the situation. The tentative man or woman consistently gets this wrong. They will take small risks but their ability to assess rewards is suspect. This is the person who plays the slots at Vegas. They are using small amounts of money hoping for the big win, but being generally satisfied with the small wins they do get. Over a period of time the slot person, the tentative, will lose it all. They get sucked into the, "I might win big" thinking and lose track of the reality that they are financially bleeding to death.

Inside the Soul of the tentative is a jumble of emotions and thoughts. The fear of losing something will deter them from placing too much of a bet, and from thrill-seeking. This doesn't have to be just related to money, it can also involve other aspects of life. How many of us have not pursued relationships with others because we were tentative about risking getting to know someone. When we don't reach out, when we are tentative, we don't lose relationships, but we do lose the potential benefit of relationships.

The Soul of the tentative contains lingering emotions, and it is these that they cling to. They don't want to lose what they do have, even the negative emotions. The negative emotions are like friends who are obnoxious; you don't like them but who would be left if they were all gone? The fear of loss of these emotions stops the tentative from taking too much of a risk. This generally means that they remain and get built on, or added to, by the new negative emotions that come up as a result of the failures which arrive when the tentative is unsuccessful in their risk-taking. I view this as a slow spiral downward into an emotional prison.

The tentative has an emotional objective too:

- To hold on to what he or she has

That is our eighth and last emotional objective. Now let's list them all together, and look at anything they may have in common.

The Emotional Objectives of Risk-Taking

Let's look now at the eight emotional objectives we uncovered in unhealthy risk-taking, and see if we can spot any patterns.

1. Validation of personhood
2. Emotional boosting.
3. Avoidance of negative feelings
4. Creating positive emotions
5. Immediate emotional self-gratification
6. The filling of an emotional void by achieving control over their life
7. An emotional high
8. To hold on to what he or she has

The thing I first noticed was the similarity in the list to the emotional objectives found in other compulsive behaviors that lead to addictions and emotional prisons. This simply leads me to the understanding that risk-taking can be as dangerous to a person's Soul as drugs or religion or pornography.

The thing that struck me most was the temporary nature of the emotional results of unhealthy risk-taking. Even the fourth and sixth objectives, which seem to offer some long-term benefits, are still only temporary fixes for trying to deal with whatever is lingering in our Souls. It suggests to me that we are designed in such a way that activities cannot ever result in feelings of importance or security.

The problem with temporary fixes is just that - they don't last. So just as with other compulsions, risk-taking leads to ongoing problems. A risk-taker gets their emotional objective met, and then the fix wears off, so they have to do it all over again. First it becomes a habit, then a compulsion, and then an addiction. At this point they are trapped in the emotional prison of risk-taking.

Let's now look at how this fits in with how we feel about ourselves with the SPAR analysis.

Risk-Taking and SPAR

As I'm sure you recall the first SPAR factor of "Security" involves how we feel about ourselves. Let's look at this in the context of risk taking.

The risk-taker is an insecure person. As you read about the derivation of the emotional objectives you probably picked up on this truth. I think this factor is the driving force behind all the dysfunctional risk-taking we see in our culture. This is certainly true for all those things I did in my youth, and even true for my choice to follow Christ. I was insecure in the deepest part of my Soul, and God drew me toward Him as I took that risk the day I accepted Christ.

What goes on inside the Soul of the risk-taker that causes this insecurity to be there and actually seem to get worse over time? As we talked about in Chapter eight of the first book, there is a dislocation between our values, beliefs and attitudes, and what we know and understand. For example, our beliefs don't match up with what we observe to be true. For risk-takers we might believe that if we just could win this bet, things would be better. Then we win the bet, and things are better for a while, then our emotional state returns to where it was. This is unsettling for the Soul; our beliefs have been invalidated by the facts. This unsettling causes our insecurities to rise up and even gain strength over time.

Just like a religion addict who begins meeting their insecurities by using some religious practices to feel better, so it is with a gambler. The compulsion begins at a minor level and grows as the emotional deficiencies never seem to quite get met. Just as with religion or drugs or perfectionism, the insecure risk-taker spirals downward slowly until they find themselves trapped in an emotional prison.

One of the characteristics of an insecure person is that they are usually not in touch with their personal insecurity. This means that although they know that something isn't quite right at a subconscious level, they probably couldn't identify it. The dislocation between the Mind and Heart, or what the individual knows and believes, is not visible. The risk-taker therefore continues to have negative emotions he or she is not in touch with and continues to try to substitute new emotions derived from taking risks. After a while the emotions generated from risky activity don't work as well, so he or she might have to increase the risk frequency or intensity to get a better emotional result. I'm sure you can see that this is how the spiral downwards gets going.

Personal insecurity is a major motivation for a risk-taker to look for ways to feel better by doing things to generate internal emotional responses. I have never met a person who ever found personal security through taking risks, and I suspect I never will. I have seen lives ruined, marriages destroyed and people dying as a result of trying to deal with personal insecurity by taking risks. Risk implies danger, and so often the danger is validated by the results of risk-taking, and people find themselves in emotional prisons.

The second SPAR factor is that of personal "Performance", and we ask, "How do I feel about myself, due to what I do?" When you ask risk-takers this question you generally get one of two answers. They are, "I feel great about what I do", and the other "I feel bad about what I do." There doesn't seem to be any neutrality. We must understand something here. The risk-taking has the same results for both groups of responders, the meeting of the emotional objectives we have already discussed. So why do we have two responses?

The difference is that the first group comes at the question from a heavily self-centered or self-absorbed perspective. Even if their risk-taking affects other people in some way, they don't care. It is all about them. The second group is a little more complex. They do have some measure of remorse about the true results of their risk-taking. They do care about how the activity is affecting them or others, which is why they feel bad. Sometimes they feel bad enough to seek help, but usually only after some significant problems have arisen where it is obvious that their actions, their performance, is the problem.

So is personal performance an important factor? Yes and no seems to be the answer to that question. Yes for those who are inclined to consider their own well-being and the well-being of others. No for those that are self-centered.

The third SPAR factor is "Acceptance." The question here is, "How do I feel about myself, due to my perception of what others feel and think about me?"

Does this factor influence a risk-taker? Not much in my opinion. The risk-taker is a person who usually listens only to his or her own counsel. That means that other people's thoughts or feelings about them are of little consequence. They tend to seek the company of other risk-takers, so that they share in each other's misery or glory. It is not really about acceptance though; it is more about empathy through shared experiences.

The last SPAR factor is that of personal "Responsibility." Our question to ask is this, "How do I feel about myself, due to my ability to meet specific standards?" Does this influence whether someone becomes and stays a risk-taker? I really don't think it is that important.

The risk-taker constantly has to challenge himself or herself with risk to achieve their emotional objectives. The idea of certain standards just doesn't fit because the standards they are using to determine how they feel about themselves are continually changing. In one situation a gambler might take a $100 bet, and next time a $50 bet. There are so many circumstantial aspects to taking risk that specific standards don't make sense.

Summarizing the SPAR analysis for the risk-taker I think we can say only one of the four factors is significant. That factor is personal insecurity, and it is this that drives the dysfunctional risk-taking behaviors we see all around us.

It is a negative testimony to the state of our country that we have so many people who are dependent on risk-taking individuals. The whole city of Las Vegas was built around it, although they have wisely diversified away from over-dependence on gambling. I don't know how much of the US economy revolves around risk-taking, but I think it is something to think about. The economics of the business is built on having people who are insecure available and acting out their insecurities by risk-taking. The industry thrives on helping people get into and stay in emotional prisons.

In this chapter we have looked at the unusual emotional prison of risk-taking, which is sometimes called gambling. We have seen that risk-takers have a variety of reasons or emotional objectives, for engaging in their behaviors. We have also seen that at the root of most risk-taking is personal insecurity.

I have also tried to give you a glimpse of my own experiences in risk-taking. It is certainly true for me that my dysfunctional behaviors in taking unnecessary risks are a result of my personal insecurities. When I do take a look back over my life I sometimes wonder how I made it past twenty without getting myself killed. I was definitely trapped in the emotional prison of risk-taking, and I'm so glad that things are better now. As I have matured, I have come to understand that it was God who was protecting me from my own folly. He saved me from death and rescued me from the potential results of my risk-taking.

A Final Word On Risk

There is an aspect of risk that is important for personal growth and for Soul healing; which I wanted to be sure to mention here. When we enter into relationships or are already in some that are not particularly deep, we must take some risks. In my risk potential explanation, this would be a risk for reward. The basic reason for this is that all humans were created for relationship. Probably the biggest risk would be to become vulnerable to others, meaning we need to take the risk of telling someone our "stuff." I will be covering this in detail later in the third book when I talk about practical aspects of healing, particularly when I cover the subject of confession.

21

OTHER PRISONS

Soft addictions are an alluring, seductive aspect of our culture - they are easy to attain and socially acceptable, they are even encouraged in many cases. Yet they are lethal to the spirit.
Judith Wright

In preparing to write this book, I realized that there was no practical way of covering all the emotional prisons I had identified. I therefore was forced to select the few that I thought had the most significance in our culture for an in-depth review. This chapter is going to cover a few more important emotional prisons in summary form. These are:

- **Work**
- **Materialism**
- **Vanity**
- **Anorexia and Bulimia**
- **Shopping**
- **Cluttering**
- **Entertainment**

Quite a list! Let's dive in.

Work

Work or workaholism is commonplace in America. In fact there are 12 step programs for self-help with workaholism, but everybody is too busy to attend. This lame joke makes a good point though; workaholics are too busy to have a life. They are so wrapped up in doing things to earn a reward that they can only allocate small amounts of time for things like their relationship with the wife and kids.

It is probably quite obvious that the workaholic is driven by personal performance criteria, the P in our SPAR analytical approach to figuring out motivations. The SPAR method asks the question, "How do I feel about myself, due to the things I do?" The workaholic answers, "Great!"

Just as we have seen in other "isms", or compulsive behaviors, the root of the overworking is emotional. The Soul contains those pesky lingering negative emotions that haven't been resolved, and the workaholic tries to mask or overcome them with the good feelings generated as a response to personal performance.

The workaholic gets on his or her hamster wheel each day with the emotional expectation that he or she will feel good after a hard day's work. They become hooked on the positive feelings they generate through work, and that is their emotional prison. They are so trapped that people who are close cannot compete for their affections. The wife and kids are left out in the emotional cold.

This emotional prison is such a strong one that it usually takes something severe to get a person out. On top of that list is losing a job. This is devastating to a workaholic as their personal identity is wrapped up in their work. Second on a list of severe circumstances would be physical inability to work due to a medical or psychological incapacitation. Third would be the loss of significant relationships, as in a divorce. Any one of these three could bring the person to what addicts call a "bottom", which could be the beginning of the healing process that will eventually get them out of their emotional prison.

Materialism

As I have mentioned before, I grew up in England, and when I was about 22, I encountered my first big materialistic moment. I was in the parking lot of a pub with some friends and I noticed an E-Type Jaguar - it was a pale yellow color and had a little bump on the bonnet (hood in American English) for the twin-carburetors. The owner came out of the pub and started the car, it purred and shot out of the parking lot, and I was in love with a thing. It was an emotional experience that I never forgot, and I think a little part of my Soul was converted into a materialist.

Back in 2000 I found myself with enough money to buy new car, and as I started the process of looking around, you can guess where I ended up. I bought a Jaguar; I couldn't get an E-Type, as they are not made now, but I did buy the top of the line model. Was I being materialistic? In this purchase I probably was, although I think of myself as generally neutral to material things. Some of us are not like that, however, and seem to be possessed by possessions.

Materialism is an emotional state in which a person spends his or her resources, mostly time, money and natural gifts, in the pursuit of material goods. While it can cover acquiring goods in all parts of a person's life, it usually doesn't. Materialism comes out in many ways. For some men it typically comes out in having all the power tools available, or all the latest electronic devices as soon as they come out, or the very newest and best golf clubs. For women it could be having the best furniture and decorations a house could need, or more shoes than she could possibly wear, or a completely stuffed wardrobe.

Materialism, which is sometimes known as consumerism, is like a religion. I defined religion like this in an earlier chapter:

- **Religion is a system of beliefs in someone or something that we have zealous faith in, where our beliefs are put into actions.**

In the case of materialism we can see all the elements of religion, a system of beliefs, a thing or things (an object(s) of worship), faith and actions. Materialists believe in their Heart something like this, "If I own these items, I will feel fulfilled." They focus on the items, or things, that seem to give them positive emotions. They have faith, a strong conviction, that the acquiring of material goods will do it for them even in the face of no proof that this is true. Of course they act out in expending time and money to get what they want.

Even though most of us would deny we are materialists, we cannot. Our whole culture revolves around acquisition and consumption. We have whole industries, like advertising, whose only function is to get us to consume. We have academic departments in our top universities dedicated to getting us to consume, marketing being the usual name. We are bombarded with messages every day about how we need a bigger house, a faster car, more alluring lipstick, a tastier burger and a brighter television. The American Dream seems no longer to be success, freedom and independence; it is whatever Madison Avenue says it is.

The thing the advertising and marketing people know is this. Our consumerism is driven by our emotional condition. Their job is to convert our emotional deficiencies or negativeness into acting out by persuading us to go and acquire their product. It is an industry that has an aspect of psychological manipulation about it.

Why do we consume so much, and why so much more than we actually need? It is because we have discovered that consuming results in good feelings in our Soul. The good feelings will often mask our feelings of inadequacy or worthlessness or ineffectiveness, the type of negative feelings that seem to weigh us down. When we come home to our big house, in our new luxury car, put on our designer sweats and plop down in front of our big screen TV, we feel good. When I describe our life that way it is easy to see how truly empty the materialist's life really is. It is empty because instead of dealing with the emotions that hold us back, we paper over them with consumption. A materialist is no different than the drunk in this; they just have a different kind of drug.

In terms of the SPAR analysis, I think Security is the big factor. A materialist feels better about his or her position when they have all their worldly goods around them. When they are not feeling secure in themselves, they can always go out and buy a new toy. To a certain extent the "R" in SPAR is also applicable. This is due to the "keeping up with the Joneses" influence that is so common in our culture. If all our neighbors have a luxury car, then so should we!

Materialism is clearly an emotional prison, and it is one that Scripture speaks against consistently. Here are two well-known scriptures that address the issue:

Lk 16:13 - No servant can serve two masters; for either he will hate the one and love the other, or else he will be devoted to one and despise the other. You cannot serve God and wealth.

Mt 12:26 - For what will it profit a man if he gains the whole world and forfeits his Soul? Or what will a man give in exchange for his Soul?

These are both quotes from Jesus Himself, and I think He speaks very clearly about the effect of wealth, or material things on our Souls. Note also that wealth itself is not condemned; it is how a person handles it that becomes the problem, or as I put it, the prison.

Vanity

Vanity is having an inflated pride in oneself or one's appearance; it is sometimes called conceit. Typically we can spot this in a person when we see it, and most of us are uncomfortable with it; even the vain people.

Just look at what we do as a society to look good. We exercise, we have plastic surgery, we get our teeth capped and we use copious amounts of make-up. Do you remember "Dress For Success" a book first published in 1975? It was a book on how a man can be vain, presented in a way to make vanity acceptable. Vanity is everywhere.

Let's be sure to state quite vociferously that all these things, the exercise, plastic surgery, teeth capping, make-up and dressing for success, are all perfectly acceptable, until they begin to run your life. It is the excesses which I am focusing on in this section of the chapter.

I'm going to go through a series of observations here, and then we'll look at what they collectively might mean. Gyms have a lot of mirrors. Day Spas are very busy. There seem to be nail salons or beauty shops in every strip center. Super-models are skinnier than ever. Most leading actors and actresses have serious workout regimens. Fashion magazines routinely airbrush their pictures. Americans spent over $12 billion on elective plastic surgery in 2008. A presidential candidate recently spent $400 on a haircut.

When I contemplate these facts, I find myself having to offer an opinion question. Don't you, the reader, agree with me that we as a group of people seem to be overemphasizing the external? There is nothing wrong about keeping one's appearance in reasonable condition, but it seems that some of us go too far in trying to perfect our image. We see imperfections everywhere; in our hair color, our body shape, our weight, our lip size, our noses, our muscle size, and I could go on, but I'm sure you get the point. We have even crossed over the line with what magazines do as they actually alter pictures with techniques designed to make the object of the picture look better in some way. The line crossing here is creating a lie about an image.

So, what is going on? On the macro level there is a social value being pushed on all of us. It is that we are to esteem how we look over how we are; or, put another way, our image over our character. At the individual level, we take this idea in through the gateway of our Soul, and internalize it as a belief. We then feel emotions in situations where our external image is concerned and we act out. This acting out can be as simple as getting our hair fixed, as obsessive as exercising compulsively, or as complex as having a complete face alteration through plastic surgery. Whenever we do these things we feel better about ourselves.

Looking at vanity through the eyes of SPAR analysis we can see some things. My primary observation is that the root of these behaviors is we are not comfortable with how we look externally. That is insecurity, the "S" from SPAR. As an example of what I mean, some people exercise frequently for their general fitness, which is healthy and is motivated by appropriate self-care. Others exercise frequently for body shape or to impress others, which is insecurity at work. Of course some people say they do it for their well-being, and are actually doing because they are insecure!

Another factor at work with vanity is the "A" for Acceptance. I mentioned impressing others in the previous chapter; this could also be the search for the acceptance of other people. We worry that if our hair is out of place, others won't accept us. Our presidential candidate with the $400 haircut was doing that. He was worried that some voters wouldn't vote for him, and would reject him.

Vanity causes some of us to work hard to present a certain image of ourselves to others. It can determine how we act, where we spend our time and money, and what lengths we will go to so that we will be viewed in a favorable way. We can develop obsessions, compulsions and even addictions around this need to be perceived a certain way. It is yet another emotional prison we can fall into if we are not careful about our values, beliefs and attitudes.

Anorexia and Bulimia

Although these are two distinct eating disorders, they have their origins in the same emotional situations and this is why I'm covering them together. The first thing to state is that both of these behavioral labels are not exactly correct. What we call anorexia is more properly know as anorexia nervosa, and bulimia is also more correctly known as bulimia nervosa. In our common use we drop the last part of the correct emotional condition wording.

Anorexia refers to the loss of appetite as a response to an internal emotional condition. Bulimia is similar; it is usually chronic and compulsive overeating accompanied by some form of self-induced vomiting and/or laxative use. The common threads in both disorders are that they revolve around food and self-esteem issues. Let's look at the origins of the two.

Immediately prior to this discussion on the two eating disorders we looked at vanity. These two problems are closely related to that emotional prison (think of them as being in the same cellblock) where prisoners with two types of similar offenses are kept together. Young people, in this case almost exclusively girls, are bombarded with messages about personal body shape and weight by our society. The gateway of their Soul is opened up to the distinct message that "if you are not thin, you have no value." I readily admit that no message says that very thing, but the total of all the messages does say it. The constant reiteration of this message leads to values, beliefs and attitudes being formed in the Heart which support this perspective.

Once these values, beliefs and attitudes are cemented in the Heart, it is only a matter of time before a young girl compares what she is and what she is "supposed" to be. Her weight and body shape become all-important in determining if she feels okay about herself. No matter how thin she is, it is likely to not be thin enough; no matter what her weight, it won't be a low enough number. There is an internally generated pressure to stay thin and keep that weight under an iron grip, fully supported by the ongoing stream of messages that confirm her values, beliefs and attitudes about thinness.

All four of the SPAR factors are at work here. The "S" for Security, may be the dominant factor since an anorexic or bulimic confuse their physical condition with their personhood. This leads to the distorted thinking that because of what they are (their shape and weight) then who they are (their person) is not good enough. This leads to negative emotions about themselves, such as inadequacy, imperfectness, and worthlessness. We can group these emotions together and see how this leads to a sense of insecurity

The "P" of SPAR, for Performance is more of a secondary factor. The person who is dealing with these two conditions knows that what they are doing isn't healthy. This is why the anorexic or bulimic often hides their condition. Knowing this adds to the feelings generated by insecurity, and makes the whole problem worse.

"A" for Acceptance is important too, but I don't think it is as significant as it might seem. The acceptance of others, or apparent lack of it, is part of the package of messages an anorexic or bulimic receives which confirm their values, attitudes and beliefs. It adds weight to the feelings of insecurity that they are already carrying around. I think of it as adding rocks to a hiker's backpack, slowing him or her down.

The last SPAR factor is "R" for Responsibility. This may be the second most important of the four factors. The anorexic and bulimic are working to a certain standard and goal for weight and body shape. This intensifies the feelings of insecurity when these self-determined goals are not met. Failure is added on to worthlessness or inadequacy, making things emotionally worse.

When all the effects of the four factors are added together the anorexic and bulimic can be seen to be carrying an enormous emotional load. The pursuit of thinness and perfect body shape dominates their thinking, feelings and behaviors. The feelings lead them into a spiral downward that often ends with serious health consequences and sometimes even death. The reason the true names of these conditions are anorexia nervosa and bulimia nervosa is because they have emotional roots. This is why they are powerful emotional prisons.

Shopping

We all have to shop, just like we all have to breathe, eat, and drink water. However, shopping is not a matter of survival, but to some it can feel that way. As I've said before, I come from England where there isn't nearly the number and assortment of shops that we have in the States. There are very few stores there even open past 6 pm, and that includes supermarkets. When I came here, shopping was a major adjustment for me, and I think that the great American fascination with going to the store has always intrigued me.

We do have to shop, we do need to keep our household running, but do we need every conceivable kind of store which seems to be open at all times? Do we need so many cable TV shopping channels or so many Internet shopping websites? All these kinds of stores are constantly available to meet our every real and perceived need. Why is this?

My answer is that America is hooked on shopping. It is an emotional prison that has some element of necessity about it, just like the "additives" we discussed in an earlier chapter. After allowing for that necessity we still shop way beyond what is sane. Some of us go shopping just to feel better. In fact some of the people who read this will admit that they are one of those people.

My thinking on this is that shopping is a behavior initiated by some kind of emotional prompt. By this I mean that a person chooses to go shopping when they feel some kind of emotional deficit such as a negative emotion from a life situation. This could happen frequently or sporadically. The shopaholic might be a regular shopper, or they might be a binge shopper, just as some alcoholics drink every day and some drink to excess when the mood arises. Of course, with shopping one can always take purchases back, but with drugs you can't.

Looking at shopping from a SPAR perspective, it seems that the compulsive shopper is dealing with the "S" for personal Security. It is when an individual is not feeling secure that they impulsively head out to the store. The other three factors don't seem to carry any significance worth discussing with this behavior.

After a few good purchases, a shopaholic can be satisfied until the next emotional prompting, except when the bills start rolling in. Overshopping, or buying unnecessary items, can often lead to conflict within a family as it damages the integrity of a budget or stretches spending power beyond the ability to generate income. Sometimes a shopaholic will hide their behavior just as a drug user will hide their activities. It is clear that shopping can be just as addictive as cocaine, which is why it is an emotional prison.

Cluttering

Did you know that there is a 12-step group called Clutterers Anonymous? Well, there is and they define clutter this way:

Clutter is anything we don't need, want, or use that takes our time, energy or space, and destroys our serenity.

All of us have at least some clutter, so my question for us is this, "Where does all this clutter we have come from?" The obvious part of the answer is that we choose to accumulate unneeded or unwanted items over time through our normal daily activities. The pack rat in us just hoards these things and they gradually take over our lives. There may be an element of materialism involved as we hold on to unnecessary possessions. This may also be a result of our overspending and not being able to part with our acquisitions. Most often, though, it is due to not being emotionally able to part with things that come under our personal control.

To me this is clearly an issue of insecurity, which corresponds to the "S" in SPAR. A clutterer is not comfortable with himself or herself unless they hang on to the things that come into their life. They feel more secure holding onto these possessions - they feel like they have more control over their life with their things around them. I read a story once about an old woman, who lived out in the country, and who had passed away without anybody knowing. When the authorities discovered her, she was slumped in a chair with over 40 years of the local daily newspaper around her. It was figured out that she had started collecting them after her husband had passed away, over 40 years earlier. This seems to be an example of a person who was suddenly faced with their personal insecurity, and chose to deal with it by cluttering.

Often we confuse clutter with mess. They are not the same! Clutter can be very organized; the old lady had her newspapers in neat piles, and her house was basically tidy. Clutter can become a mess, but doesn't have to be. We have all seen pictures of houses with cars up on blocks in the front yard, an old washing machine next to it and trash everywhere. That is both clutter and a mess. So when is clutter not a mess? My answer is this; have you seen how many personal storage units we have in America? Apparently our houses are not big enough for our stuff, and we need more space in which to keep it. That is often due to clutter.

The problem with clutter is that as it accumulates it starts to cause us to have to spend more time on dealing with it, more money on storing it and more effort in dealing with it. It actually becomes a physical and emotional drag on our lives. Temporarily, our cluttering assuages our personal insecurity, but then we run into the feelings which spring up in our Soul due to our choice to hoard this mostly useless stuff. We mask our feelings of insecurity with the cluttering, then we add on new negative feelings, such as anxiousness, making our emotional condition worse. It is similar to getting a fix from a drug, only to find we feel worse off after the drug wears off.

I knew that I just had to put this verse of Scripture into this little section of the book. My wife is a very organized person; it is one of the things I really appreciate about her. She is fond of reminding me that "God is a God of order", and she has this verse among others to back her up:

1 Cor 14:40 - But all things must be done properly and in an orderly manner.

I like to point out to her that some people can be very orderly but accumulate a lot of clutter, like the old lady in the story. That is where the word "properly" in the scripture becomes important. We must get rid of the things we don't need, as they encumber us in living a fuller life. If we don't make that choice, we are choosing the alternative, the emotional prison of cluttering.

Entertainment

The dictionary provides us with an enlightening definition of "entertainment." It says that entertainment is, "amusement or diversion provided especially by performers." The key word in this definition is 'diversion." Remembering that, let's also look at what "entertain" means. The same dictionary says it is, "to keep, hold or maintain in the Mind." In the context of how the Soul works, keeping, holding or maintaining in the Mind in our definition means to "occupy our thoughts." Putting these two things together we can see that entertainment can be used to divert the internal activity of the Soul. Divert it from what? From dealing with the thoughts and feelings of our regular life. We use entertainment as an emotional distraction.

Most of us experientially understand this. If we are feeling low we might chose to watch a comedy movie or if we are stressed we might want to see an action flick. When we are feeling relationally needy, a chick flick seems to help, and sometimes we just want to veg out or get away from it all by turning on the TV. All of these actions are demonstrating a basic idea we have seen throughout the book. We often get stuck in an emotional prison by dealing with our negative emotions through a compulsive behavior.

In the case of entertainment, we pay others to provide amusement, which distracts us from feeling our negative feelings. For some of us, receiving entertainment through the gateway of our Soul is like getting a fix or having a couple of cocktails. It achieves the same thing, it temporarily stops us from feeling things we don't want to. Just like all the other emotional prisons we have discussed, it is only a temporary fix.

In the context of SPAR analysis, we can see that if entertainment is used as a "fix", then someone is dealing with how they feel about themselves.

This is the "S" for personal security. It seems to me that the other three, performance, acceptance and responsibility, are not that influential in choosing to self-medicate with entertainment.

There are some interesting positive aspects to entertainment, which I ought to mention so that we don't get too negative about it. Entertainment can be used effectively to change our perspective on situations. For example, if we're going through a rough experience and we see a movie about "overcoming the odds", we might realize that we have hope. Some of the entertaining that occurs on in children's hospitals is about providing hope. When the USO goes to entertain the military overseas, they are providing connection with the homeland, which helps the troops handle being isolated more easily.

Here's a positive use of entertainment that maybe nobody has thought of. When we go to church we usually have some kind of service that has music, a form of entertainment, in the early part of the worship time. One of the reasons is that it helps the congregation to put aside the things of life which are dragging them down emotionally, and replace them with feelings toward and about God. This allows the message to be more effective than if you had no music. This is why churches with no music or boring music will not be effective in promoting changed lives through changed Hearts. When the attendees don't connect with the entertainment, their Souls aren't ready to receive the word of God so easily.

Scripture speaks to this, even though most people don't recognize in the way I have discussed it. In the Bible there are several references to "singing a new song." One particular verse which demonstrates this is:

Ps 96:1-2 - Sing to the Lord a new song; Sing to the Lord, all the earth. Sing to the Lord, bless His name; Proclaim good tidings of His salvation from day to day.

One of the reasons God tells us to sing new songs is this; He knows, and so do we if we consider it, that culture, including personal entertainment choices, changes over time. For Him to reach us most effectively, godly music will need to keep in step with the culture. People who are one generation younger than me will need different entertainment to prepare their Souls for God's messages than I do. Churches that choose to continue doing the same thing for 50 years are destined to lose their ability to reach the lost, because the lost won't connect with their entertainment. The message of the church needs to stay the same, and that is the Gospel of Christ, but the entertainment needs to be up with the times.

Even church music can be used to distract us from our feelings. Sometimes I just like to sit and listen to contemporary praise and worship music, especially when I'm driving alone or getting ready to go to church. I use it as a sort of soother for my day, or to prepare myself to receive God's word. If I took this to the extreme, I would be doing the same as a person who constantly watches movies or TV. I would be distracting myself and my emotions, thereby getting a fix.

If this challenges you a little, that is good. This is what I suggest; turn off the TV for a week and see how you feel. Your emotional response will tell you if you use entertainment to get a fix. If your emotional response is very big, you are probably trapped in the emotional prison of entertainment. That is when you might want to seek help by talking to safe friends or even some form of a counselor to find out what is at the root of your negative feelings.

A Last Word

That's it for this chapter. We have gone through, in an outline form, several more emotional prisons. There are many more which we could discuss. All we have to do is pull up a list of compulsive behaviors or addictions from the Internet and we can find more.

In the next chapter I'm going to provide a short overview of the subjects we've covered in the last several chapters. This is to consolidate our understanding of emotional prisons before we move on to how to deal with them, which I call the "healing" section of the three books.

22

SOME OBSERVATIONS

Reason, Observation and Experience, the holy trinity of science.
Robert Green Ingersoll

This is a short chapter. This where I look back at the last few chapters, in which I describe actual emotional prisons and their origins, and make some overarching observations. This is the chapter of transition from looking at the problem to looking at the solution.

The Universality Of A Problem

My first overarching observation is this: Every human being is faced with dealing with difficult emotions. There is no culture, nation, social group, tribe, or family; which is untouched by the problem of how to handle their emotions.

We have seen how one person not handling their emotions properly can lead to the death of millions of people. All the most infamous dictators who became mass murderers were psychologically challenged by their own emotions. Part of their answer to their emotional problems was to murder others, and that took the complicity of other emotionally dysfunctional individuals to accomplish. All of the political, military, religious or social leaders in history who used murder to gain and consolidate power were driven by their negative emotions. I can't tell you which emotions were involved in each case, but I can tell you that there were mixtures of some the following: worthlessness, rejection, inadequacy, powerlessness, imperfection, anger, shame, guilt, failure and many more.

We have seen how one person's inability to deal with difficult emotions leads to their many dysfunctional behaviors. Abuse, the use of pornography, prostitution, alcoholism, drug addiction, and excessive gambling can all be traced back to the mishandling of negative emotions. Even so-called socially acceptable dysfunctions such as workaholism, people-pleasing, and perfectionism have their roots in the same issue, emotions running a person's life.

The whole of human history, both personal and collective, can be shown to be a product of how we handle our emotions. Just to show where it began let's look at the moment it started. We have already looked at this situation in an earlier chapter, so I'm only going to spend a moment on it. Let's look at the book of Genesis:

Gen 2:25 - And the man and his wife were both naked and were not ashamed.

If you recall the story, they rebelled against God's simple instruction, they became aware that they were naked, and the negative emotion of shame was introduced into their lives. This was the moment that all of us, their descendents, became subject to the power of negative emotions in our lives. A good question to ask here is why? Why did God create these negative emotions that Adam and Eve, and subsequently all of us, experience? I will be answering this at the end of this chapter when I discuss the purpose of emotions.

The problem of dealing with negative emotions is one which all humans in all cultures and societies around the world have to handle. Every individual you ever meet has to do it, and so do you and I! This is a universal problem.

Do Emotions Mislead Us?

Most people would answer "yes" to this question, especially with the knowledge that how we deal with them leads us into what I have called emotional prisons. My answer, though, is "no." The answer to this question is my second overarching observation.

Part of our response to any situation is the generation of emotions within our Souls. This response is a designed reaction within the Soul; it is part of how God has made us. I'm not saying that each of us will have the identical reaction to any given situation, just that we will have an emotional response. We need to dig into this a little more to understand what is happening within each human.

In Chapter Eight of Book One "Emotional Prisons – Origins", the chapter where I introduced SPAR analysis, I spent some time on answering the question, "Where do feelings come from?" Our emotions are internally generated by the Soul as a response to a situation. They are mostly influenced by our values, beliefs and attitudes; I'll define all three to facilitate this discussion.

Value – A principle, standard or quality regarded as worthwhile or desirable.

Belief - A mental acceptance of, or conviction in, the truth or actuality of something.

Attitude – An inclination of the Heart, sometimes called a state of Mind or feeling.

Importantly, values and attitudes are subjective in nature, while beliefs are objective. We all tweak some of our values and attitudes, probably on a daily basis. We don't alter our convictions of truth, our beliefs, without a major reason. Sometimes our beliefs are so concrete in nature that we will choose to die rather than give them up. It is the beliefs lodged in our Hearts that influence our emotions more than any other Soul characteristic. This is what is fundamentally important about understanding the integrity of emotions.

So, do emotions mislead us? The answer is that they seem to, but the reality is different. It is our beliefs that primarily influence which emotions are generated within our Soul. We then act out based on these emotions. However, it is the beliefs we hold that are the real culprit in whether we seem to consistently make bad choices as we act out of our emotions.

God, who designed us, knows this, which is one of the reasons He constantly warns against unbelief in Him. He knows that not believing in Him and His Scriptures will lead to more dysfunctional life. Believing in Him leads to a life of freedom, freedom from being trapped by our emotions.

The overarching observation here is that false beliefs lead to false or dysfunctional emotional responses. These responses then lead to bad choices, which then lead to impulsive and compulsive behaviors, which often lead to emotional prisons.

Should I Fear My Feelings?

Since we tend to get into trouble in life through acting out of our emotions, should I be afraid of them? The answer to this question will be my third overarching observation.

My answer to this is "yes", though not the debilitating extra emotion of fear that will freeze a person up, or paralyze them from action. The fear to be recognized here is the respectful fear, such as a small child might have for a parent. Just as a small child will embrace a parent we must embrace our emotions. Let's see why.

Emotional responses are designed into us; we have been given them by God for a reason. All emotions have purposes, which I'll be discussing later in this chapter. One of the purposes is to tell us something; The problem is that if the basis for our emotions is wrong, in other words our false beliefs, then we might indeed be led astray as we discussed in the previous section. Throughout the last few chapters you read about people dealing with negative emotions in less than sensible ways. That is being led astray.

Knowing that due to our beliefs and the resulting emotions we might err in judgment should lead us to understand that a healthy fear, a respectful fear of those emotions is entirely appropriate.

The overarching observation here is that there is not enough cautious respect given to what we feel, and this is part of the reason we get into so many dysfunctional behaviors so easily.

The Building of Emotional Prisons

I have talked several times in the previous few chapters about people spiraling downward in an emotional prison. Another word picture I like is that of building emotional prisons. This is my next overarching observation.

My wife and I recently took a trip to England with two of my grandkids, boys aged 14 and 15. One of the days was a trip to visit Stonehenge and some castles. One of the older castles was actually a ruin, and we could see some of the rooms from the walls, one of which was a dungeon. It was deep and I had the boys climb down into it for picture taking. Then they had to climb out, and that wasn't so easy! The dungeon was deep and walled with flint like stone, and that made it hard to get out. This is how I imagine a psychological prison might be - deep and hard to get out of. For the record, the boys did get out.

None of us gets into an emotional prison overnight, it isn't one strike and you are out. It isn't even three strikes and you are out. It is a slow and building movement. It starts with the building of the perimeter wall, just like one of those castles. We act out in minor ways, such as dishonoring our parents or vandalism as adolescents, and we add a rock or two to the wall. Eventually the wall gets built. After that, or even at the same time, as our compulsions become more specific or intense, we start to build the walls of our jail cell, our dungeon.

As time goes by we add cement to the rocks or bricks of our acting out, place more pieces into the walls, and we build it from the inside. One day we are fully trapped, we are deep in our dungeon. We might realize it, or we might not, but whether we do or not, we are just as trapped. If we continue in our acting out we will simply add to the walls, making them thicker. As the walls get thicker, we start to get more and more emotionally choked, and put ourselves in a place where it is hard for us to reach out for help. Some of us even delight in being trapped, saying something like, "That is the way I am." Even if we try to climb out we are always trying to scale emotionally flinty rocks, which can tear us up as we climb. It is a difficult place to be, emotionally speaking, and seems to be a dungeon of hopelessness.

Emotional prisons are built brick by brick. They don't get put into place quickly, and we build them ourselves, even though we may blame others. That is my fourth overarching observation.

Some of us end up in Multiple Prisons

Not only do we build our own emotional prisons, but also some of us build prisons with multiple layers. This is another very common problem and is my next overarching observation.

Almost anybody with experience in the field of compulsive behaviors, both as the person acting out and as a psychologist or social worker, will agree with this. Rarely does a compulsive person only have one "ism." They almost always have at least two, and in my experience, three compulsive behaviors they are dealing with. When we sit back and reflect on this it actually makes sense.

As we have repeatedly said, these compulsive behaviors originate from the mishandling of emotions. It is very feasible that someone who is struggling with dealing with their feelings might develop more than one avenue of escape from them or different ways of self-medicating. For example a people-pleaser may also be a rabid shopper and a secret drinker. In groups I have been involved with I have repeatedly seen this kind of situation.

Multiple issues is one of the reasons that therapy should not be rushed; often the first problem is not the only one. It is also the reason that when some people enter therapy, they actually start to feel worse. This is because more dysfunction is being revealed. It ought to be expected and a good therapist will know and understand this, and explain it to new counselees as normal but healthy. It is healthy because old problems which are revealed can be addressed and dealt with; problems that are not revealed continue to cause trouble in a person's life.

What happens then is that not only do we build our dungeon brick by brick, but it can have multiple layers of walls by the time things get totally out of control in our lives. That is the overarching observation.

I'm not a "fill in the blank"

I'm not an alcoholic, I'm not a sex-addict, I'm not a perfectionist: These are all statements made by people who are exactly what they say they are not. I imagine we've all come across people who are acting out and say that they are not. This is called denial.

If you were a betting person, you could safely bet your entire life savings on this one. The person acting out will always deny it when confronted. Since I'm going to cover this subject in detail in the chapters about barriers to healing in the next book, I won't say more here, except for this: Denial is always present in the life of someone trapped in an emotional prison. It is part of their emotional defense mechanism where they attempt to deny that something is wrong.

Troubled people will always deny their coping dysfunctions. That is the sixth and last overarching observation.

193

The Purpose of Emotions

Just to be sure we understand something basic about emotions, we must first look at what the word emotion means, as this will help us develop our understanding of their purpose. The word "emotion" is derived from the French verb "emouvoir", which itself is derived from the Latin "emovere." Both of these original words carry the meaning "to stir into action." That is what emotions do; they stir us into action. This is exactly what we have discussed several times, but in the context of acting out of our emotions in dysfunctional ways.

There are many, many, theories on the purpose of emotions. If the psychology profession can't definitively decide the reason for emotions even existing then how can we expect to understand them? To address this issue of the purpose for emotions, I propose we go back to the situation that existed before the fall of man.

In the beginning mankind was fashioned out of the dirt after God spoke the creation into existence. The account of this is found in Genesis Chapter One and Two. At that time Adam and Eve were in perfect harmony with the world God created, God Himself and each other. The only clue we have about emotions is that apparently Adam and Eve were "not ashamed." Even this one thing tells us a lot!

First, we know that God has not changed the physical or psychological design of mankind since he made Adam and Eve. This means that all the emotions we, all mankind, experience, were designed into us from the beginning. Adam and Eve therefore would have been able to feel both negative emotions such as shame or guilt or confusion, and positive feelings such as happiness, adequacy and contentment.

Second, Adam and Eve were not in a state of shame, meaning that shame wasn't lingering inside their Soul. Even though they may have felt shame, it didn't remain in them.

Third, they experienced intimate fellowship with God as they went about the garden.

Just picture it! Whenever Adam and Eve had a question about what they were feeling, they turned to their creator for an answer. So whenever either of them experienced a negative emotion, they knew God had an answer for it, and it was never allowed to linger within the Soul. In fact there is evidence in Scripture that God, in His graciousness, takes our negative emotions and replaces them with positive ones. Here is one example:

Jer 31:13 - For I will turn their mourning into joy, and will comfort them and give them joy for their sorrow.

These things point us to a very simple conclusion. Negative emotions have a purpose of directing us to God to get them resolved. While we are not too concerned with positive emotions, I will address them too. Positive emotions also have the purpose of directing us to God, but to enable us to share our joy with Him who created us and to be able to thank Him for giving them to us.

Emotions do many things for us; for example they help us see danger, they help us deliver messages to others, and they signal that we need to deal with something. These things, which are often wrapped up in the theories about why emotions exist, are all secondary, but important, aspects of our psychological design. The primary reason for the existence of emotions is that they are part of how we are to connect to God.

My view on this is backed up in the first part of the next chapter (in Book Three, Emotional Prisons – Healing) when we explore the first "principle of healing", which is that God is the source of all healing.

Let's Get Healed!

The first chapters of this book series detailed the origins of the problem of emotional prisons, and of how and why we get ourselves into them. In the next book, we come to the message of hope. There is a way to get out of the traps we get into. It can be thought of as a jailbreak, but I think it is better approached as a demolition. The walls of the emotional prison can be torn down; nobody has to stay in their dungeon. I am calling this process "healing."

Appendix A

Books and Other Resources mentioned in Emotional Prisons.

In Book 2 – Emotional Prisons - Prisons

<u>Chapter 13.</u>

The Quran, University of Michigan translation.

The River War – Sir Winston Churchill. (1899 version)

The Arab Mind – Raphael Patai

<u>Chapter 14.</u>

The Jesus Seminar, an organization.

Christianity In Crisis – Hank Hanegraaff, chapter on dysfunctional Christianity.

Love and Respect – Emerson Eggerichs.

<u>Chapter 15.</u>

Addicted to Love – Stephen Arterburn. (Not referenced, but still a good book to read on the issue of false intimacy.)

God's Grace and the Homosexual Next Door – Alan Chambers.

Intimacy needs resources:

1. Parenting with Intimacy (Workbook suggested) by Dr. David and Teresa Ferguson, Dr. Paul and Vicky Warren and Terri Ferguson.
2. Discovering Intimacy Workbook, by Ferguson and Walker.
3. Go to www.greatcommandment.net for a more complete listing.

The Search for Significance – Robert McGee

Chapter 16.

Yale study mentioned is reported in Journal of Pediatrics, Feb 1996 by William Tamborlane M.D. et al. of Yale University.

Chapter 18.

Co-dependent no more – Melody Beattie.

Co-Dependence – Healing the Human Condition by Charles L. Whitfield.

http://www.codependents.org/ The CODA worldwide website.

Chapter 20.

Mere Christianity – C. S. Lewis

Chapter 21.

Dress For Success – John Molloy

http://sites.google.com/site/clutterersanonymous/Home The website for people dealing with clutter that offers a 12 step solution.

In Book 3 – Emotional Prisons - Healing

Chapter 26.

Shame – The Exposed Self – Michael Lewis

Chapter 28.

Safe People – Henry Cloud and John Townsend.

Celebrate Recovery – www.celebraterecovery.com

Al-Anon - www.al-anon.alateen.org

Appendix B

Scripture References used by Chapter

In Book 1 – Emotional Prisons - Origins

Chapter 1. - 2 Pet 2:9, Gen 1:26-27, Jn 4:24, Mk 12:30, Mt 28:19.

Chapter 2. - Isa 55:8-9, 2 Tim 3:16-17, Jas 1:17, Mt 23:23, 1 Sam 15:29, Pr 1:7, Pr 9:10, 1 Kings 4:29.

Chapter 3. - Mt 22:36-40, Ps 119:105, Rom 10:9-10, Jn 14:6, Jer 12:3, Ecc 11:9, Jer 17:9.

Chapter 4. - Gen 2:16-17, 1 Cor 7:5, 2 Pet 1:5-8, Gal 5:23-23, Mt 11:27 (Lk 10:22), Jn 14:6.

Chapter 5. - Mal 2:16, Dt 31:6.

Chapter 6. - Pr 4:23, Jer 17:9, Col 3:21.

Chapter 7. - Eph 5:11-13, Lk 17:1-2, Ex 20:14.

Chapter 8. - Ex 20:3-17.

Chapter 9. - Jas 1:8, Rom 15:7, Pr 22:6.

Chapter 10. - Mt 7:24-27, Gen 2:21-24, Gen 2:18, 2 Cor 6:14, 1 Cor 15:33.

Chapter 11. - None.

In Book 2 – Emotional Prisons - Prisons

Chapter 12. - Dt 18:9-12.

Chapter 13. - Dt 7:6, Gen 12:2-3, Jn 11:47-53.

Chapter 14. - Rom 3:23, Heb 11:1, Eph 2:8-9, Mt 28:18-20, Eph 5:33, Eph 6:12, Ps 8:4.

Chapter 15. - Jn 10:30, Jn 17:20-23, Lev 18:22, Pr 6:16-19, Job 31:1-3.

Chapter 16. - 3 Jn 2, 1 Cor 6:19-20.

Chapter 17. - Gen 4:13-14, Gen 4:6-7, Pr 29:18.

Chapter 18. - Rev Ch 6, Jdg Ch 14-16, Gal 1:10.

Chapter 19. - Col 3:23.

Chapter 20. - Mt 25:14-28, Mt 16:26.

Chapter 21. - Lk 16:13, Mt 12:26, 1 Cor 14:40, Ps 96:1-2.

Chapter 22. - Gen 2:25, Jer 31:13.

In Book 3 – Emotional Prisons - Healing

Chapter 23. - Ex 15:26(d), Ps 41:4, Ps 103:3, Ps 107:19-20, Ps 147:3, Isa 53:4-5, 2 Ki 5:1-14, 2 Cor 12:7-9, Jn 5:5-6, Jas 5:13-16, 1 Cor 12:28.

Chapter 24. - 1 Ki 11:4, Ecc 12:13-14, Mt 11:28-30, Jer 6:16, Jn 16:33, Mt 7:24-27, Pr 14:27, Pr 16:25, Mt 4:4, 2 Chr 7:14, Rom 10:9, Lk 5:25-26.

Chapter 25. - 1 Jn 1:6, Jn 12:37-40, Isa 6:9-10, Pr 16:18, Dan 4:37, Ps 86:5, Mt 6:12, Mt 6:14-15, Ps 32:3-5, Ps 69:29.

Chapter 26. - Gen 2:25, Gen 3:7-10, Ex 20:2, Ex 20:3, Isa 58:11, Jer 31:25, Eph 6:12, Eph 6:13, Ecc 4:9-10, Isa 43:18-19, Isa 5:13-14, Pr 1:29-33, Eph 4:30-32, Mt 6:15.

Chapter 27. - Lk 5:17, Pr 9:10, Isa 11:2-3, Acts 9:31, Pr 10:27, Pr 14:26, Pr 14:27, Pr 16:6, Pr 19:23, Pr 22:4, Pr 2:1-5, Ps 119:11, 1 Cor 2:14, Lev 26:3(a), Lev 26:11-12, Phil 2:8, Josh 24:14-15, Jer 17:9, Pr 4:23, Lam 3:40, Jn 8:31-32.

Chapter 28. - Ps 32:5, Jas 5:16, 1 Jn 1:9, Gal 6:2, 2 Cor 5:16, 2 Cor 7:10, Pr 11:14, 1 Cor 15:33, Pr 13:20, Isa 32:6, Pr 17:12, Mt 22:39.

Chapter 29. - 2 Cor 10:5, Pr 22:7, Jn 8:44, 2 Cor 10:5 (Msg), Heb 4:12, 1 Cor 10:13, Eph 5:33, Jas 4:3, Ps 77:5-6, Phil 2:12-13, Eph 4:22-24, 1 Cor 15:31 (Amp), Rom 12:2, Lam 3:40.

Chapter 30. - Rom 3:23, Isa 53:6, Jas 4:1-2, 2 Tim 3:16-17.

www.ingramcontent.com/pod-product-compliance
Lightning Source LLC
Chambersburg PA
CBHW060500290526
45791CB00001B/202